Take care this Day of Valentine,
That you are not mistaken.
And like the Lovers that fell out,
And lost the flitch of Bacon.

EXPLANATION.

When A Couple went to claim the Flitch of BACON at
DUNMOW, they were just going to take it away but the BAG
being found too little the wife said I told you so we have had a
Thousand words about it, and so lost the BACON.

THE
HISTORY
OF THE
DUNMOW FLITCH
CEREMONY

by

FRANCIS W. STEER

F.S.A., F.R.Hist.S.

Senior Assistant Archivist

Essex Record Office

With a Foreword
by
J. W. ROBERTSON SCOTT, C.H., Hon.M.A.(Oxon.)

Published by
THE ESSEX COUNTY COUNCIL, CHELMSFORD
ESSEX RECORD OFFICE PUBLICATIONS, NO. 13

Printed by
J. H. CLARKE & CO., LTD., CHELMSFORD

1951

A

FOREWORD

WITH happy memories of my life at the end of the last century near Dunmow (at Great Canfield) where I invented that pioneering rural author, ' Home Counties '; wrote the first two or three of my dozen and a half books ; had among my neighbours and friends writing men like de Vere Stacpoole of *The Blue Lagoon*, S. L. Bensusan, whose Essex stories we relish, H. A. Gwynne, editor of the defunct *Morning Post*, and R. D. Blumenfeld, of the *Daily Express*, with the kind and gracious Countess of Warwick, the witty Tom Gibbons, who so continuously defended the bacon, William Hasler, who so genially sold corn and bricks, and Harold Munro and Harold Begbie, whose books we valued— they were both tenants of mine—and Hastings Worrin, who knew so much about local history, I have been greatly interested in this impressive volume which residents in and visitors to Dunmow owe to Mr. Steer's scholarship and assiduity.

That is a long sentence, but this is a long book which puts my little sixty-four page *Story of the Dunmow Flitch* in the shade. I have, however, a distinction that Mr. Steer has not got : I have been the Prior of Dunmow at a Flitch ceremony!

May the decent historic fun of Flitch days continue to be displayed by many generations of Dunmow people! May few of those days be wet! May plenty of twelve-and-sixpences from Essex folk at home and abroad, and visitors on the merry occasions, acknowledge our debt to Mr. Steer and all the helpers he has had.

J. W. ROBERTSON SCOTT

Idbury Manor, Kingham, Oxford.

CONTENTS

LIST OF ILLUSTRATIONS

Line-blocks in text   PAGE

PREFACE

The outline of the story of the Dunmow Flitch custom is known in every English-speaking country; it is one of our institutions with an origin so lost in antiquity that we can only examine such evidence as is available and consider which of the legends—if indeed they are only legends—is the one from which the custom was derived. This is the primary aim of this book. Secondly, the time has come to record details of the winners of the Flitch from the earliest times to the present day when the ceremony has degenerated into a mere entertainment for the masses in many parts of the country—and abroad—and is no longer confined to its rightful home. Lastly, I have attempted to bring together all the miscellaneous references to the custom which have been found during several years research.

The passing of the old manorial system with its cumbersome legal machinery has destroyed much of what was picturesque in England, but such sweeping reforms are inevitable in this present age of speed and uncertainty. Perhaps some people will say that it would have been better if the Flitch ceremony had been decently buried and forgotten after a claim was refused by the lord of the manor in 1772. We cannot, under our changed circumstances, enact the ceremony with all its former solemnity, but should we not grasp at a justifiable excuse to retain some pageantry in our lives even if we are only playing? The preservation of an accurate account of over eight hundred years of Essex history centred round one tiny village is important, and this year, the two-hundredth anniversary of the last legitimate award, seems an appropriate one for this record to be presented.

Some years ago, Mr. J. W. Robertson Scott (late editor of *The Countryman*, that green-covered quarterly which has done so much to preserve the spirit of rural England), wrote a small book entitled *The Strange Story of the Dunmow Flitch* in which he gave the cream of the history in his own inimitable style. Mr. Robertson Scott's book is now scarce, so I hope he will forgive me if I have modelled this present work partly on his researches. Although one writer does not like to pirate another's work, it could scarcely be avoided in this instance, and I would therefore like to make full acknowledgment to Mr. Robertson Scott both for the information and pleasure which his book gives. The inclusion of his portrait and a Foreword from his able pen are other tokens of his generosity.

I am also indebted to Mr. Alfred Hills, F.S.A., that distinguished Essex antiquary, who gave me all his notes on the Dunmow Flitch ceremony some years ago. Likewise I am grateful to Mr. T. G. Luckin and other Great Dunmow residents who have lent me pictures and programmes of old Flitch trials, and given me much help in other directions. I must also record my thanks to Colonel T. Gibbons, D.S.O., D.L., J.P. (who will long be remembered as counsel for the defence of the bacon), for giving me a number of details not obtainable elsewhere and allowing me to reproduce his portrait in a typical pose, and to Mrs. H. J. Chiswell, of Great Easton, who, in her indefatigable searches for local historical information, has brought many Flitch items to my notice. My thanks are likewise due to the Editor of the *Essex Chronicle* for giving me access to his files, and to the many correspondents, known and unknown, who have so kindly answered my questions. It is again my duty to record the debt due to my colleagues, Mr. F. G. Emmison, F.S.A., and Miss H. E. P. Grieve, B.E.M., B.A., who have given me the benefit of their advice at various stages in the production of this book.

The Dunmow Rural District Council gave facilities for the painting (*Plate XXVI*) in their custody to be photographed, and the Dunmow Parish Council were equally kind in allowing me to reproduce two pictures (*Plates X, XXV*) belonging to them. The Trustees of the British Museum granted permission for *Plates V, VI, XVII, XXII(b)* to be made from photographs of records in their collection, and I wish to acknowledge the help I have received from the Departments of Manuscripts and Coins and Medals. Thanks are also due to the Controller of H.M. Stationery Office and to the Secretary of the Royal Commission on Historical Monuments for permission to reproduce *Plates IV, XXVIII*. The photographs for *Plates XX, XXII(a)* were taken by Mr. H. F. Hayllar, of Hoddesdon, who has given his valuable collection of Essex prints and negatives to the Record Office.

My greatest debt is to Mr. G. W. Worrin, of Hertford, who gave me the entire collection of Flitch papers formed by his father, Mr. Hastings Worrin, and himself. I know what a sacrifice this entailed, but as a true lover of Essex and its history, Mr. Worrin would not deny a large public of the information so carefully preserved over long years.

Patmers, Duton Hill, Great Dunmow.   FRANCIS W. STEER

x

CHAPTER I

THE BACKGROUND

Little Dunmow is an Essex village with about four hundred inhabitants. It is approximately thirty-seven miles from London, two miles east of Great Dunmow, and twelve miles from Chelmsford if approached through Felsted. As the name Dunmow implies—the meadow on the hill, or hill meadows—the parish is situated on high ground. The village is watered by a tributary of the Chelmer, and has an area of some 1,728 acres of which most are arable ; it is made up of a few houses on either side of the Great Dunmow—Felsted road, half a dozen farms, and the church. While the surrounding country is attractive, Little Dunmow has no claim as a beauty-spot, and would be but seldom visited were it not for its historical associations.

At the time of the Great Survey made in 1086, Little Dunmow was held by Ralph Baynard who had no less than twenty-five lordships in Essex alone as his reward for services to William the Conqueror ; his grandson, William, was deprived of this vast inheritance for his share in the rebellion against Henry I. The Baynard territories were then given to Robert, a younger son of Richard FitzGilbert (or FitzRichard), from whom descended the celebrated family of FitzWalter of whom no less than ten generations held Little Dunmow. It was not until the death of Elizabeth, widow of Walter FitzWalter, in 1464, that this great family's estates were to be divided. Little Dunmow came to the share of Elizabeth, only daughter of Walter and Elizabeth, and the wife of John Radcliffe (whose grandson was created Earl of Sussex in 1529) ; the estate remained in that family until the death of Robert, the last Earl, in 1629.

1

Historians are a little hazy about the early years of the priory which features so prominently in this story, but its foundation may be said to date from 1104 when Juga Baynard, commonly known as the Lady Juga, caused Maurice, Bishop of London, to dedicate the church of Little Dunmow to the honour of the Virgin Mary. Two years later, Lady Juga's son, Geoffrey, obtained licence from Anselm, Archbishop of Canterbury, to place canons in the church, so it is to these two that the establishment of the priory as a house of Augustinian Canons may be credited. Lady Juga had given half a hide of land to the church at its dedication, and Geoffrey added further lands and tithes. When the Baynards lost their estates, the priory's position was precarious, but fortunately Robert FitzRichard and Maud his wife not only confirmed the foundation, but increased its resources by further grants of property and tithes. Thus the possessions of this religious house grew steadily, and were advanced by successive members of the FitzWalter family until, in 1291, the temporalities were valued at £40 19s. 2½d. a year.

The priory, although never of major importance, continued to flourish, and appears to have been a manor in itself because, after the dissolution, Henry VIII granted to Robert, Earl of Sussex, the site of the priory, and the ' manor of Priory Place, Little Dunmow, late the Priory ' (see *Plate I*). At the time of its dissolution in 1536, the priory was worth £173 2s. 4d. a year gross, and £150 3s. 4d. net ; the buildings were valued at £83 10s. 8d., the cattle at £19 16s. 2d., corn at £62 1s. 4d., and 206¼ ounces of plate at £38 4s. 11d., this latter sum being little more than the debts of the house which were reckoned at £34 4s. 3d.

But we are not so much concerned with the priory as a religious house as with the unusual custom with which it was so closely united.

CHAPTER II

THE ORIGIN OF THE FLITCH CUSTOM

The Flitch custom is of such a great age that it is doubtful whether we shall ever discover how it really started. Several theories have been advanced, and they all deserve consideration. The most popular and incorrect version is that created by Harrison Ainsworth whose long poem, *The Custom of Dunmow*, relates how Sir Reginald FitzWalter and his wife, disguised as humble folk, went to the priory and begged for the prior's blessing a year after their marriage. Sir Reginald is made to say :

> In peasant guise my love I won,
> Nor knew she whom she wedded ;
> In peasant cot our truth we tried,
> And no disunion dreaded.
> Twelve months' assurance proves our faith
> On firmest base is steadied.

The prior, impressed by the devotion of this young couple, hailed the convent cook who was carrying a flitch of bacon on his back, and presented it to the lovers. Sir Reginald then revealed his identity, and gave lands to the priory on condition that a flitch should be given to any couple who were prepared to make an oath that they had not repented of their marriage for a whole year.

Sir William Dugdale, the seventeenth-century herald and antiquary, gives this account in his *Monasticon Anglicanum* :

Here was an ancient Custom, according to this old saying, viz. That he which repents him not of his Marriage, either Sleeping or Waking, in a Year and a Day, may lawfully go to Dunmow and fetch a Gammon of Bacon. That there was such a Custom is certain, and that the Bacon was deliver'd with much Triumph and Solemnity. This continu'd till the Dissolution of the Abby and the Party claiming was to take his Oath before the Prior and Convent and the whole Town, humbly kneeling in the Church-Yard, upon two hard pointed Stones, and the Ceremony being long, it must be painful to him . . . . . Some had a Gammon, and some a Flitch, in Proof whereof it appears by the Records of the House . . . . . it appears to have been a Donation of some conceited Benefactor, and there is no doubt but that, at such a Time, the Neighbouring Towns and Villages resorted, and were Partakers of their Pastimes.

3

Neither does Philip Morant, the Essex historian, writing in 1768, enlighten us when he says :

It does not appear who instituted this custom ; but, it is generally thought, it was one of the family of FitzWalter. The Prior and Canons were obliged to deliver it [the bacon] to him that took the oath, by virtue, we may believe, of some injunction of a founder or benefactor, by which they held lands, rather than their own singular frolick and wantonness : or, most probably, it was imposed by the Crown, either in Saxon or Norman times, and was a burthen upon the estate, as the same custom was at Wichenor in Staffordshire.

But the words, ' either in Saxon or Norman times ', used by Morant are important, and provide a clue to a probable origin of the custom which is far older than the period of the FitzWalters. We may disregard the remark that the Crown had anything to do with imposing the conditional obligation to provide a flitch or gammon if demanded, but we cannot overlook the fact that the solemn ceremony of marriage, as understood (even if not observed) today, was not regularly complied with until comparatively late in history. The casual way in which people lived as man and wife in Saxon, and in earlier and later times, undoubtedly caused the ecclesiastical authorities some concern, and their approval of a couple willing to swear an oath that they were living happily together and had no reason to regret their action after a stipulated period, may have given rise to the custom of making an award. In other words, there was an inducement to uphold the sanctity of marriage, or the union of such persons who were likely to provide reasonable security for their children. So far as Little Dunmow and a few other places were concerned, the prize was bacon, and we must now consider why this particular form of reward was chosen.

Here, indeed, we have to go back a long way in history, and in the process we find that such cherished legends as the Dunmow Flitch, the Babes in the Wood, and many others, are not indigenous to our country. In the case of the bacon, the story is at least as old as the time of Virgil ; Joseph Spence (1699-1768), the friend of Pope, and author of *Polymetis*, a treatise on classical mythology published in 1747, wrote of Alba Longa (nowadays Castel Gandolfo in the Alban Hills twelve miles south-east of Rome and tradition- ally founded c.1152 B.C.) where Æneas met the white sow and thirty piglets, and mentions that Dionysius Halicarnassus recorded that a fine flitch of bacon was kept in the chief temple there, even to Augustus' time, in honour of the goddess of fertility of which the sow and her litter were emblematical.

That the pig was venerated in England is shown by its appearance on early British coins illustrated by J. Y. Akerman in his
numismatic papers ; neither can the antiquity of place-names
derived from words meaning, or connected with, pig, be ignored.
Even today, we can buy gold or silver pigs at a jeweller's shop
to be worn as charms, and before the late war, Viennese chimney-
sweeps—themselves a symbol of good luck—used to carry squealing
sucking-pigs through public restaurants on 31 December so that
their hairs could be plucked by the guests. Lucky coins bearing
an image of a child—a chimney-sweep's apprentice—riding on a
pig were sold in their thousands to the midnight merrymakers in
the Stefansplatz.

Dr. William Bell wrote at length on the folk-lore of the flitch
in *Shakespeare's Puck* (1872), and cited several instances throughout
Europe, so it is not unreasonable to suppose that the veneration
of the pig and the preservation of a part of that animal either as a
reward for virtue or in readiness as a sacrifice to the appropriate
deity in the time of trouble, was but another of those pagan prac-
tices adapted to serve a purpose among Christians. Perhaps there
was an element of truth in the remark of a labourer at the time of
the 1877 'trial' at Dunmow when he ventured the belief that
'Them ancient foaks—maybe the Rumans—guv' a bit o' bacon
to them as didn't whop their missus '.

While some of the romance of the Dunmow custom may be
destroyed by giving prominence to these ancient references, perhaps
the reason for it is made clearer. It may also be noted that the
word 'pigsney' was formerly used as a term of endearment to a
girl ; it is simply 'pig's eye', the eye being one of the most precious
possessions of an animal held, as we have seen, in the highest
esteem. Thus we have in *The Miller's Tale* :

> Hir shoes were laced on hir legges hye ;
> She was a prymerde, a pigges-nye
> For any lord to leggen in his bedde,
> Or yet for any good yeman to wedde.

As mentioned above, the custom of awarding bacon is not
confined to Dunmow, or even to this country. At Wichnor, a village
between Lichfield and Burton-on-Trent, a wooden flitch is shown
above the great fireplace in the Hall. Here the custom seems to
have originated as part of the tenure by which Sir Philip de Somer-
ville held the manor from Edward III. Morant gives the Wichnor
oath which should be compared with that demanded at Dunmow
and recited on p. 15 :

Here ye, Sir Philip de Somervile, Lord of Wichenour, maynteyner and gyver of this Baconne, that I *A.* sythe I wedded *B.* my Wife, and sythe I hadd hyr in my kepyng, and at my wylle by a yere and a day after our mariage, I wold not have chaunged for none other, farer ne fowler ; rycher ne powrer ; ne for none other descended of gretter lynage ; slepyng ne waking at noo tyme ; and yf the seyd *B.* were sole and I sole, I wolde take her to be my wyfe before all the wymen of the worlde, of what condiciones soever they be, good or evylle, as help me God and hys Seyntys, and this flesh and all fleshes.

It will be seen that Sir Philip was described as ' the maynteyner and gyver ' of the bacon, which indicates that the custom originated before his time.

At Vienna, a flitch used to hang beneath the Red Tower with these lines appended to it :

> Befind' sich irgend hir ein mann
> Der mit der Wahrheit sprecken kann
> Dass ihm sine Heurath nischt gerowe
> Und fürcht' sich nischt vore sine frowe
> Der mag desen Backen herunter howe

which may be translated :

> Is there to be found a married man
> That in verity declare can,
> That his marriage him doth not rue,
> That he has no fear of his wife for a shrew,
> He may this bacon for himself down hew.

Dr. Bell quotes the story of a claimant for the Vienna flitch who, when a ladder was brought to enable him to cut down the prize, asked that someone might do it for him, because if he got grease on his Sunday clothes his wife would scold him. The gate-keeper told him to be off ; a man who fears is certainly not master at home, certainly rues his marriage, and has no claim to the bacon. Similar instances of a quarrel about taking the bacon away is shown in the *Frontispiece,* and by Dr. Plot when describing the Wichnor custom.

At the abbey of Saint Melaine in Brittany, it was said that ' there had been hanging, for more than six centuries, a side of Bacon still quite fresh, which had been set apart for the first pair who for a year and a day had lived without dispute and grumbling and without repenting of their marriage '. The story of the flitch at Saint Melaine has not been recorded in such detail as the other examples mentioned above, but there can be no question that awarding the bacon for conjugal felicity is something far older than is popularly supposed, and the suggestions that the custom is merely a monkish prank or the joke of a king or Norman over-lord may be dismissed.

PLATE I

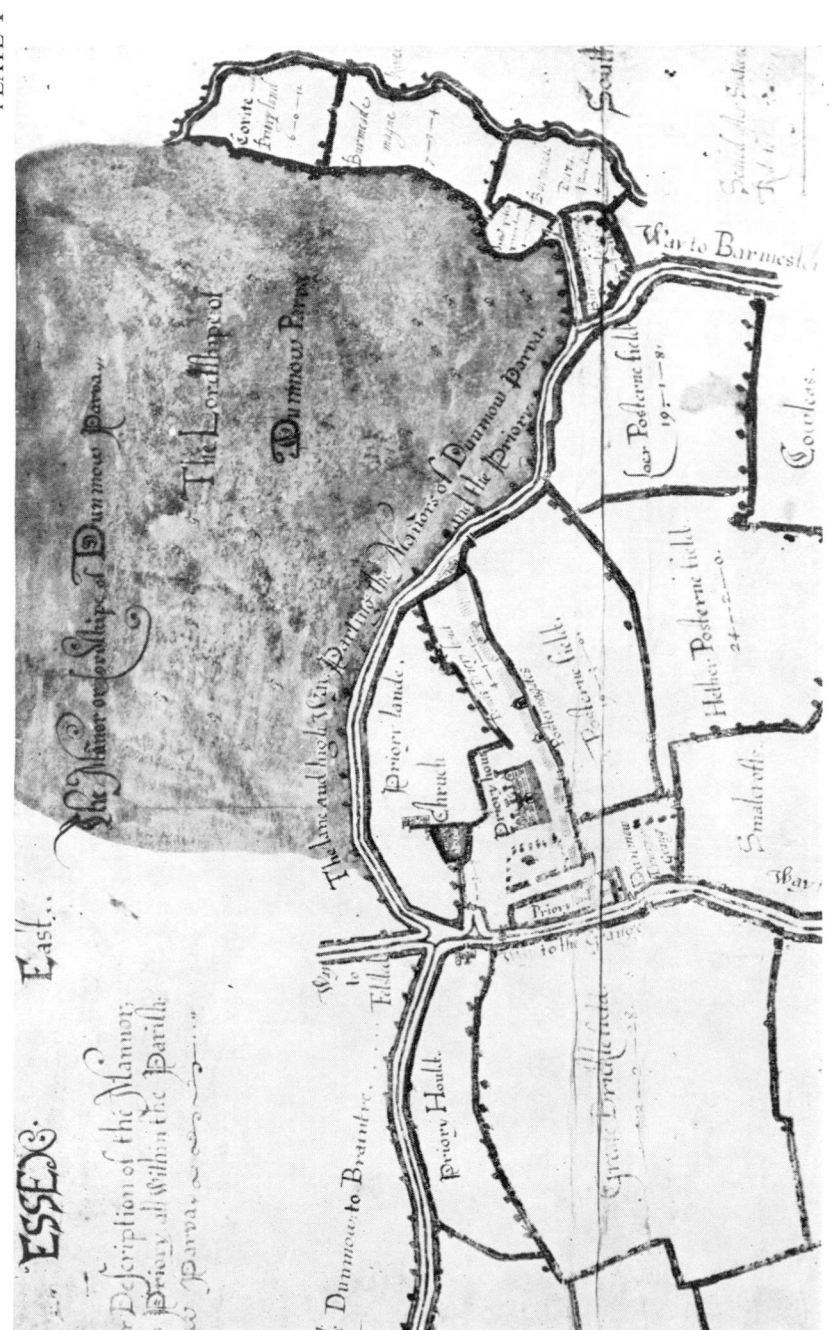

LITTLE DUNMOW IN 1631

Part of "The Plott or Description of the Mannor of Dunmow Priory", measured and surveyed by Samuel Walker.

PLATE II

THE SOUTH-WEST VIEW OF LITTLE DUNMOW PRIORY CHURCH, 1786

PLATE III

THE REMAINS OF LITTLE DUNMOW PRIORY CHURCH FROM THE SOUTH-EAST

From an Engraving by S. Lacey, 1832

PLATE IV

The Interior of Little Dunmow Priory Church

The Tomb of Joan (Devereux), wife of Walter, Lord FitzWalter, who died in 1409, is in the foreground.

CHAPTER III

THE FLITCH IN LITERATURE AND DRAMA

Shakespeare does not seem to have made any reference to the Flitch, and it is surprising that such a popular story should not have claimed the attention of more writers in Elizabethan and Stuart times. Our earliest quotation is from William Langland who flourished between about 1330 and 1400 and gave details of his life and times in that great work *The Vision of Piers the Plowman* where we find :

Meny peire sitthe the pestilence-tymw	Many a couple since the time of the pestilence
han plight treuthe to louye	Have plighted truth to love,
Ac thei lyen lelly	And they in fact lying
here nother loueth othere.	Neither of them loveth the other.
The frut that thei bryngen forth	The fruit that they bring forth
aren meny foule wordes ;	Are many foul words ;
Thei han no children bote cheste	They have no children but strife
and choppes hem by-twyne.	And disputes between them.
Thauh thei don hem to Donemowe	Though they go to Dunmow
bote the deuel hem helpe	(Unless the devil help them)
To folwen for the flicche	To try for the flitch
feccheth thei hit neuere ;	They will never steal it
Bote thei bothe be for-swore	Unless they both be perjured
that bacon thei tyne	That bacon they lose

Next in age comes good Geoffrey Chaucer (1340?-1400) from whose *Miller's Tale* we have already quoted. In the *Prologue* to the *Tale of the Wife of Bath,* we have that much-married, loose-tongued dame announcing :

> The bacoun was nat fet for hem, I trowe,
> That som men han in Essex at Dunmowe.

In 1445, when *Reliquiæ Antiquæ* appeared, the unknown writer was bewailing the corruption of standards of conduct, and while discoursing on the Seventh Commandment regrets that he could

> fynd no man now that wille enquere
> The parfyte wais unto Dunmow ;
> For they repent hem within a yere,
> And many within a weke, and souner, men trou ;
> That cawsith the wais to be rough and over-grow,

7

That no man may fynd either path or gap ;
　The world is turnyd to another shape.
Beef and moton wylle serve welle enow ;
　And for to fetch so ferre a lytil bacon flyk,
Which hath long hanggid, rusty and tow ;
　And the way, I telle you, is comborous and thyk,
And thou might stomble, and take the cryk [i.e. break your neck] ;
　Therefore bide at home, whatsoever hap,
Tylle the worlde be turnyd into another shape.

Our next example is from the pen of one Howell, a sixteenth century writer whose method of expression, even if uncomplimentary, no doubt appealed to his readers. His advice was :

　　Do not fetch your wife from Dunmow
　　For so you may bring home two sides of a sow !

It is not until the eighteenth century that we get any more literary references to the flitch. In 1778, a 'ballad opera' by Henry Bate was produced at the Haymarket Theatre by William Shield under the title of *The Flitch of Bacon;* it is not of very high quality, and Mr. Robertson Scott has selected the most appropriate verse :

　　Since a year and a day
　　Have in love roll'd away,
　　　And an oath of that love has been taken,
　　On the sharp pointed stones,
　　With your bare marrow bones,
　　　You have won our fam'd Priory bacon.

In 1783, between 25 April and 7 June, a company of His Majesty's Servants from the Theatres Royal visited Chelmsford, and on 28 May *The Flitch of Bacon* was received with great applause and repeated in the following week. It was also performed by the Norwich Company at Colchester on 17 September, 1779 and again on 30 August, 1786 ; it remained a stock piece until the beginning of the nineteenth century. After the third performance of *The Flitch of Bacon* at the Theatre Royal, Covent Garden, in 1780, when the principal characters were acted by Mr. Leoni, Mr. Reinhold, Mr. Wilson, Mr. Fearon, Mr. Edwin and Miss Brown, the following verses were contributed to the *Morning Chronicle* by an admirer of the Misses Harper and Brown :

　　Long and deservedly the Town
　　Approv'd their winning fav'rite Brown,
　　　And own'd her sprightly art ;
　　But gentle Harper's magick strain,
　　A warmer tribute shall obtain,
　　　A tribute from the heart.
　　To Brown we give the sportive thought,
　　With whim, desire, and fancy fraught,
　　　What beauty can incite ;
　　But Harper's plaintive notes improve,

The captur'd soul to modest love,
To rational delight.

The one enchants the frolick throng,
With all the wond'rous power of song,
This praise is claim'd and given ;
Here voice and feeling shall combine,
To give a transport that's divine,
And lift the soul to Heav'n.

Among a collection of glees in my possession is one entitled

A Favourite Glee

Sung by Mr Bannister Mr Brett and Miss Harper in the

Flitch of Bacon

Set by Michael Este 1600

but the words refer to the happiness of soldiers so long as they can see their Colours fly, and appear to be of late composition and set to an earlier tune.

Bate, one of the more celebrated Essex parsons, was a former editor of the *Morning Post,* a satirist and dramatist, friend of the Prince of Wales, and a pugilist of no mean order. After his release from prison in 1781 for a libel on the Duke of Richmond, he bought the advowson of Bradwell-juxta-Mare, spent £28,000 on the church, vicarage and lands, and in 1797 presented himself to the living, but being charged with simony was refused institution by the Bishop. Bate took the additional surname of Dudley in 1784, and was created a baronet in 1813. *The Flitch of Bacon* was the first of Shield's musical productions to be staged, and this led to his appointment as composer to Covent Garden Theatre, which post he occupied until 1791 when he resigned. Dying in 1829, Shield was buried in the south cloister of Westminster Abbey.

Another play, *The Devil at Dunmow,* or *Harlequin and the Flitch of Bacon,* was performed at Sadler's Wells on 20 June, 1831.

We are again indebted to Mr. Robertson Scott for the preservation of four lines, produced in 1803, and supposed to be a farmer's reply as to how he got the flitch :

I'll inform you, my friend, how it come.
You yourself will acknowledge the reason is clear,
As soon as I tell you that my pretty dear
Has been all her life—deaf and dumb !

Lovers of Dickens will recall the Lammles in *Our Mutual Friend* and their quarrelsome manner in private but affectionate attitude when anyone else was present. Dickens faintly disguised Dunmow when he wrote :

And dear Mrs. Lammle and dear Mr. Lammle, how do you do, and when are you going down to what's-its-name place—Guy, Earl of Warwick, you know—what is it ?—Dun Cow—to claim the flitch of bacon.

Mr. Bernard Shaw introduced a reference to the flitch in the Preface to *John Bull's Other Island* when, referring to the Egyptian troubles of last century. He says that the setting up of native courts had 'about as much to do with the actual government of the fellaheen as the annual court which awards the Dunmow flitch of bacon has to do with our divorce court'.

Although it can scarcely be classed as a literary reference, this counting-out rhyme known as *Harum Scarum, Dunmow Flitch,* dating from the middle forties of the eighteenth century, is worthy of preservation. A true rhyme of this type consists of a Main Count and Ejection, and the Dunmow one is :

Main Count : Thummum and Plummum and arms a-twitch.
Scotch me, catch me, coach-and-horse
Hide in heather, hide in gorse.
Ejection : With a Hey Down, *Down* !
There goes my *Gown* !

A selection of songs and rhymes, chiefly of nineteenth-century date and of questionable merit, is given in Chapter XI.

CHAPTER IV

RECORDS OF AWARDS UP TO 1751

He that repents him not of his marriage in a year
and a day either sleeping or waking,
May lawfully go to Dunmow and fetch a gammon of bacon.

From the works of early writers we have seen that the Dunmow custom was well-known, and we might have expected that
even in those days of restricted travel there would have been a
fairly large number of claimants for the bacon. It is somewhat
surprising to discover that, including the award made in 1751,
only six cases are known of the prize being won.

The first of which we have any record is that to Richard
Wright, a yeoman, of Bawburgh, near Norwich, a village famous
as the place where St. Walstan the Confessor was born. Walstan's
story is not commonly known, but briefly, he was of gentle birth,
and at twelve years of age renounced his patrimony and entered
into service at Taverham, nearby.

The young Walstan was credited with performing many
miracles, and his master, wishing to make him his heir could
persuade him to accept nothing but the calf of a certain cow. In
due season, this cow had two bull calves which Walstan carefully
brought up at an angel's command as they were to lead him to the
place of his burial. Mowing one day with his fellow labourers,
Walstan received a heavenly warning of his approaching end, and,
calling on his master and fellows, commanded them to put him in a
carriage and yoke the two oxen to it. Having given instructions that
nobody was to direct the animals on their journey, Walstan ' earn-
estly beseeched God, that every labourer that had any infirmity
in his own body, or any distemper among his cattle, if he came out
of devotion and reverence to visit his body, and to ask remedy of
God there, might obtain his desire and have his petitions granted '.
Thereupon Walstan expired, the oxen set off on their journey and,
needless to say, went to Bawburgh where a spring issued forth
at their first stopping-place ; a little further on, they made a full

11

stop and the body of the holy man was buried. A church was built over his grave as a shrine, and many miraculous cures were performed there. Walstan, who is said to have died in 1016, is the patron saint of farm labourers, and his crowned figure, barefooted, and holding in one hand a sceptre and in the other a scythe, may still be seen on some Norfolk rood-screens.

And so from this village associated with a saint, came Richard Wright to another parish which boasted of an equally famous tradition, and in the Cartulary of Dunmow Priory in the British Museum, we find this record, reproduced on *Plate V*, which may be translated, with modern punctuation :

Memorandum, that one Richard Wright, of Bawburgh next Norwich, in the County of Norfolk, yeoman, came here and pleaded for the bacon of Dunmow on the 17th day of April in the 23rd year of the reign of King Henry VI, after the Conquest, and was sworn according to the form of the gift aforesaid, &c. before John Canon, then Prior of this place aforesaid and the Convent of the same place, and may other neighbours, and there was given to him, the same Richard, one flitch of Bacon, &c.

This was in 1445, many years after Langland's reference quoted on p. 7. Twenty-two years were to elapse before another award was to be recorded and this is also found in a document in the British Museum (Harl.MS.1177). In modern characters and with the contracted words extended, it reads :

Memorandum, that one Stephen Samuel of Little Aston in Com' Essex, husbandman, came to the priarie of Dunmaw on our Ladie Daye in Lent in the 7th Yeare of King Edward 4th and required a Gamman of Bacon and was sworne before Roger Rulcok [should be Bulcott] the Priar and the Convent of this place as alsoe before a multitude of other Neighbours, and there was Delivered unto him a Gamman of Bacon.

Little Easton is only a few miles from Little Dunmow, and we shall have occasion to refer to it again when dealing with the later history of the Flitch ceremony. By the time the next award was made, Henry VIII, in his full bloom of early manhood and with no thought of dispensing with religious houses, had been on the throne less than eighteen months. Another record in the priory Cartulary is shown as *Plate VI*, and is, in English :

In the year of our Lord, 1510, Thomas the fuller of Coggeshall in the County of Essex came and pleaded for one gammon of the bacon of Dunmow, that is to say on the 8th day of the month of September, on Sunday, the second year of the reign of King Henry the Eighth, after the Conquest, And was sworn according to the form of the gift and before John Tyler then prior of this place aforesaid and the Convent of the same place and many other neighbours And there was given to the same Thomas one gammon of Bacon.

Nearly two centuries were to pass before Dunmow was to have another gala-day, but in what changed circumstances. The greed of Henry VIII had had to be satisfied and the monasteries were spoiled, the uncertain days of Edward VI and of his tragic successor, Lady Jane Grey, had to be faced ; martyrs—many of them from Essex—were burnt under Mary. The great days of Elizabeth, the reigns of the first James and the first Charles, the miseries of the Civil War, the decline of the Stuart dynasty under Charles II and James his brother, the coming of William of Orange, were all to leave their mark on the pages of history before another gammon was sought after in Dunmow, but this time, from a layman's hands instead of those of a reverend prior. Whatever may have been the course of the nation's destiny, and however it may have affected the inhabitants of this little Essex village, the Flitch was not forgotten, and on the twenty-seventh day of June in the year 1701, this manorial ceremony was duly recorded—partly in Latin—but here given entirely in English from a surviving document :

Dunmow late the Priory	At a Court Baron held for the worshipful Thomas May, knight, on Friday, the twenty-seventh day of June in the year of the reign of our Lord William III by the Grace of God King of England, Scotland, France and Ireland, Defender of the Faith, &c., the thirteenth, in the year of Our Lord 1701, before Thomas Wheeler, gent., steward of the same.

Elizabeth Beaumont
Henrietta Beaumont
Annabella Beaumont   }   Jury
Jane Beaumont
Mary Wheeler

Firstly, we find and present that John Reynolds, gentleman, and Anne his wife have been married for the space of ten years last past, and that they are persons qualified to receive the Bacon of Dunmow according to the Custom of the Manor.

Item : we find and present That William Parsley and Jane his wife have been married three years and upwards and that we do adjudge and present them to be fit and qualified persons to receive the Bacon of Dunmow according to the Custom of the Manor.

William Parsley was a butcher of Great Easton, and John Reynolds was steward to Sir Charles Barrington of Hatfield Broad Oak. A copy of the Court proceedings were printed in *The Weekly Journal or Saturday's Post*, 3 October 1724, in vol. xxi of the *Gentleman's Magazine* (1751), and in Mr. Robertson Scott's book, *The Strange Story of the Dunmow Flitch*, but the actual court-roll has disappeared and only the draft remains.

Defoe, better known as the author of *Robinson Crusoe* than of the *Tour through the Eastern Counties* which he made in 1722, tells us that he cannot remember reading that anyone ever came to demand the Flitch, ' nor do the people of the place pretend to say, of their own knowledge, that they remember any that did so ; a long time ago several did demand it, as they say, but they know not who ; neither is there any record of it, nor do they tell us, if it were now to be demanded, who is to deliver the Flitch of Bacon, the Priory being dissolved and gone '.   From this account we can only presume that Defoe did not persevere in his enquiries. The *Tour* eventually embraced the whole of Great Britain, and enjoyed a wide popularity ; each edition was 'improved' by successive editors, and later issues recite the awards to Parsley and Reynolds.

The last public award of the bacon made by a lord of the manor was in 1751 when the fortunate couple were Thomas and Ann Shakeshaft of Wethersfield. Thomas was a weaver, and his 'trial' is said to have attracted five thousand spectators which makes us wonder if this was an attempt to revive the custom and make an excuse for a fair. The official papers dealing with Shakeshaft's claim are preserved in the Essex Record Office and take this form :

Dunmow late the Priory	The Court Baron of Mary Hallet Widow Lady of the said Mannor there holden for the said Mannor on Thursday the Twentieth day of June in the Five and Twentieth Year of the Reign of our Sovereign Lord George the Second by the Grace of God of Great Britain France and Ireland King Defender of the Faith and in the Year of our Lord One Thousand Seven Hundred Fifty and One Before John Comyns Esquire Steward of the said Mannor

Homage	Wm. Townsend Mary Cater John Strutt Martha Wicksted James Raymond Eliza Smith	Sworn	Daniell Heckford Catherina Brett Robert Mapletoft Eliza Haselfoot Richard Birch Sarah Mapletoft	Sworn

At this Court It was found & presented by the Homage aforesaid That Thomas Shakeshaft of Weathersfield in the County of Essex Weaver and Ann his Wife have been Married for the Space of Seven Years and upwards and that by reason of their Quiet, Peaceable, tender, & loving Cohabitation during all the said time they are fit & Qualified to be admitted by the Court to receive the Ancient & Accustomed Oath, whereby to intitule themselves to have the Bacon of Dunmow delivered unto them According to the Custom of the said Mannor Whereupon the said Thomas Shakeshaft & Ann his Wife being present here in Court in their proper persons humbly prayed that they might be Admitted to take the Oath aforesaid And Thereupon the said Steward with the Jury Suitors & other Officers of the Court proceeded with the usual Solempnity to the Ancient & Accustomed Place for the Administration of the Oath and delivering the Bacon aforesaid (that is to say) to the Great Stones lying near the Church Door within the said Mannor, Where the said Thomas Shakeshaft & Ann his Wife kneeling down on the said Stones, the said Steward did Administer unto them the following Oath to wit

PLATE V

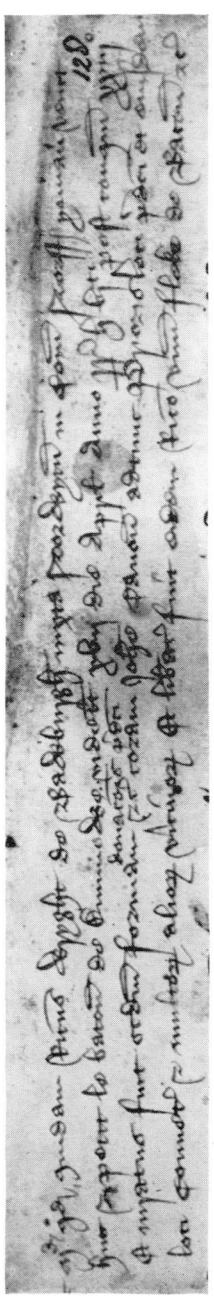

The Record of the Award of the Bacon to Richard Wright, of Bawburgh, Norfolk, in 1445, from the Cartulary of Dunmow Priory in the British Museum (Harl.MS.662).

M^d q^d quidam Ric'us Wryght de Bawburgh iuxta Norwycu' in Com' Norff' yoman venit huc & petit le bacon de Dunmowe videl't xvij die April' Anno r' r' h' vj^{ti} post conq'm xxiij^o Et iuratus fuit sed'm formam donac'o'is p'd'ci &c' coram Joh'e Canon adtunc Prioris loci p'd'ci et eiusdem loci Conve't' & multor' alior' vicinor' Et lib'at' fuit eidem Ric'o unu' fleke de Bacon' &c'

(For translation, see p. 12.)

PLATE VI

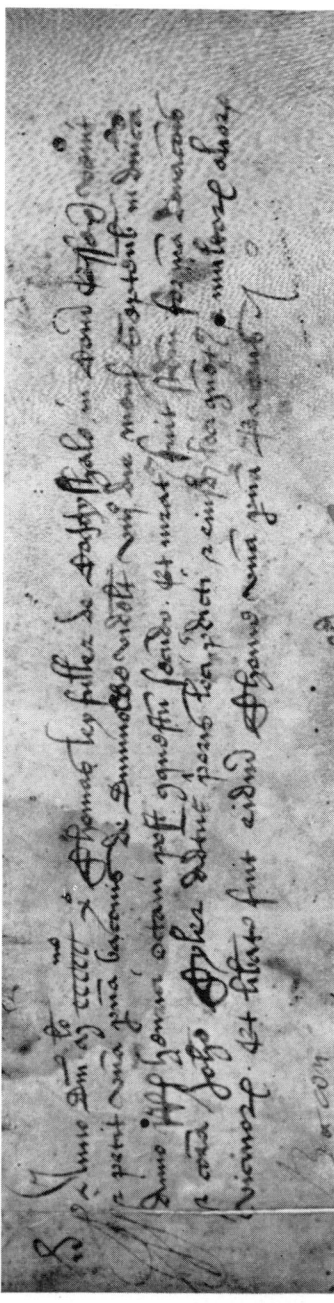

The Entry in the Dunmow Priory Cartulary recording the Award of the Bacon to Thomas le Fuller, of Coggeshall, in 1510.

¶ Anno D'ni M['o] CCCCC[mo] X[o] Thomas ley fuller de Coggyshale in Com' Essex' venit
& petit una' p'na' baconis de Dunmowe videl't viijo die mens' Septenb' in d'nica
Anno r' r' Henrici Octavi post c'questu' secu'do. Et iurat' fuit scd'm forma' donac'o'is
& cora' Joh'e Tyler adtu'c p'oris loci p'dicti & eiusd' loci c've't' & multor' alior'
vicinor'. Et lib'at' fuit eid'm Thome una' p'na' Baconis.

(For translation, see p. 12.)

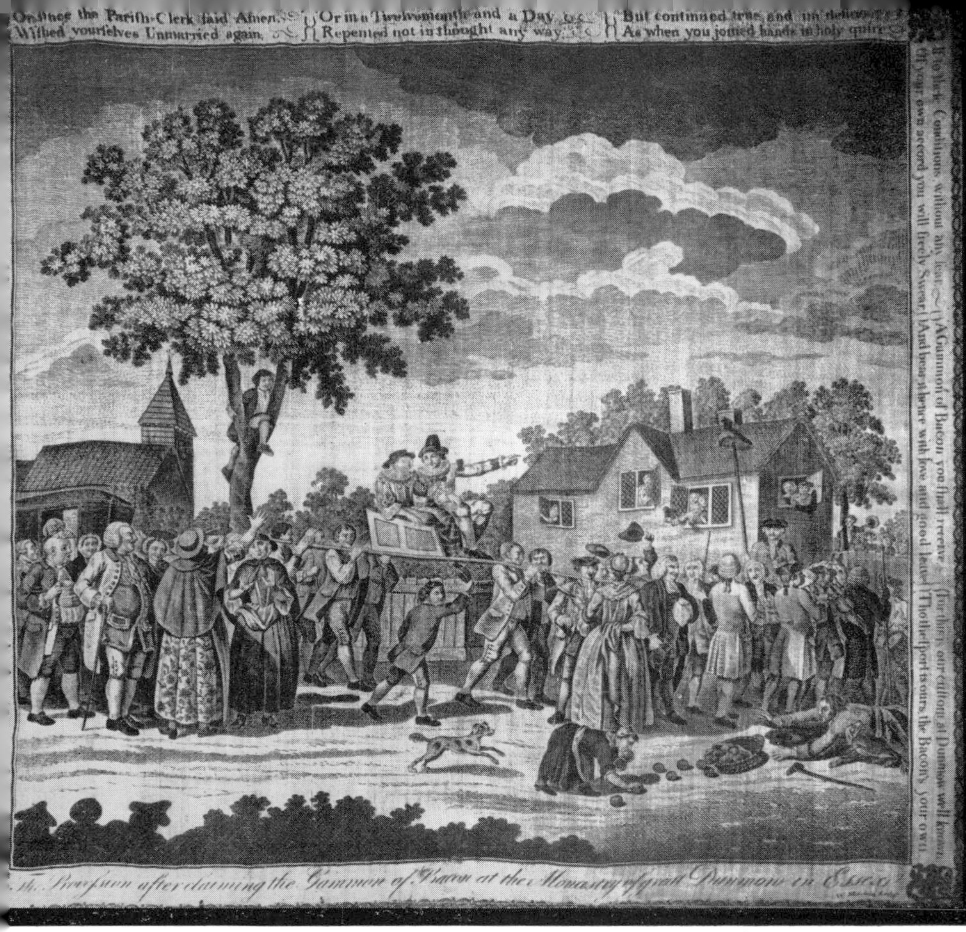

The 1701 Procession printed on a cotton handkerchief. It was on this scene, depicted by W. Sherwin, that Ogborne based his more familiar picture of the Ceremony held half a century later.

Wee acknowledge the Receipt of the Bacon according to the abovewritten Certificate

Wm Parsley
Jane Parsley

Jn Reynolds
Anne Reynolds

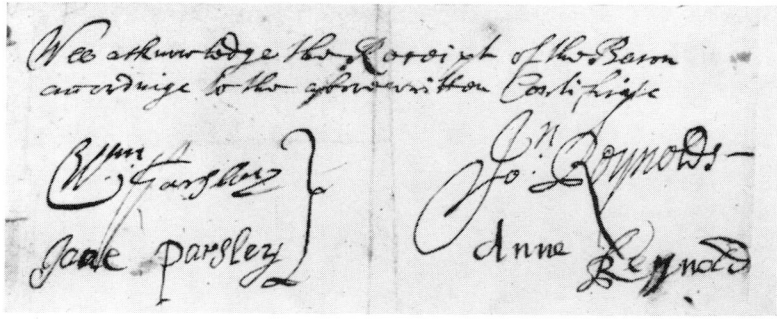

Receipts signed by William and Jane Parsley, and John and Anne Reynolds, for the bacon they won in 1701.

PLATE VII

PLATE VIII

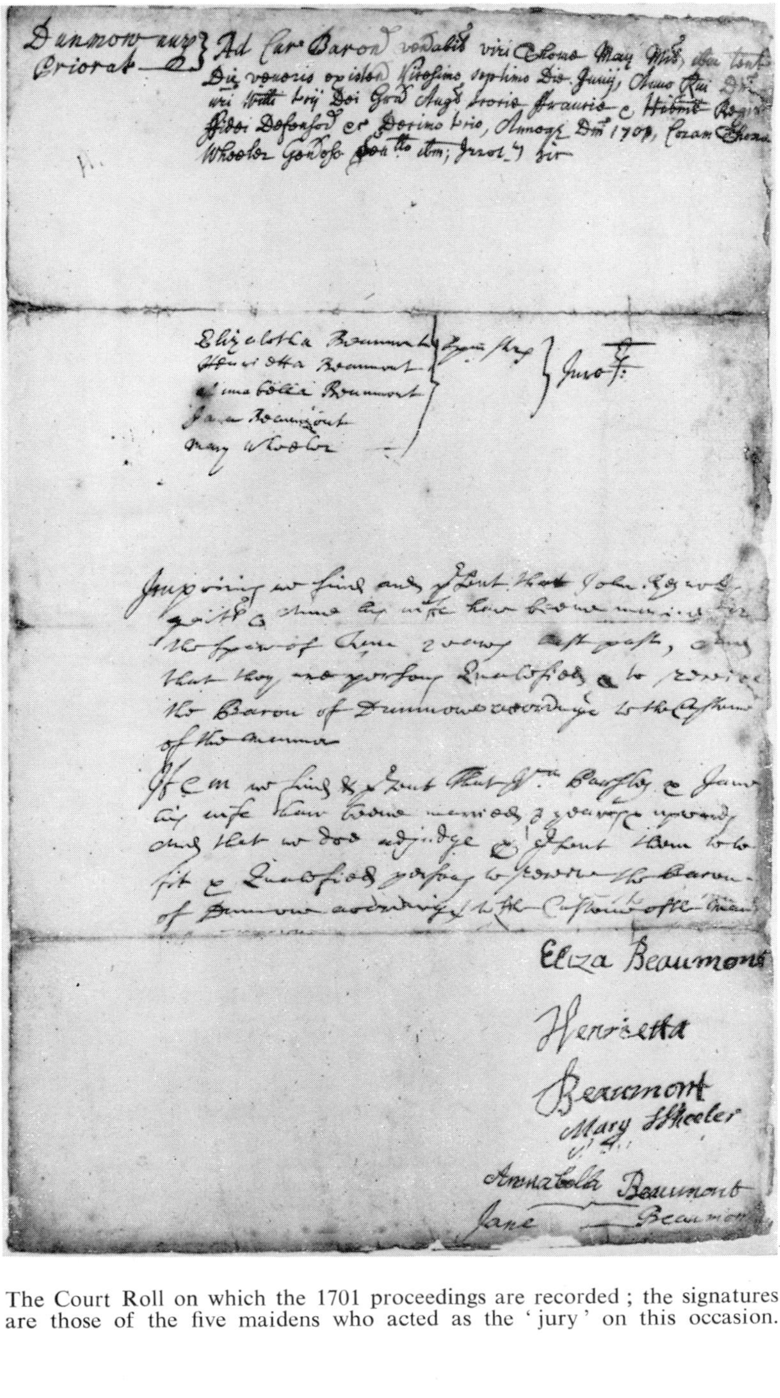

The Court Roll on which the 1701 proceedings are recorded; the signatures
are those of the five maidens who acted as the 'jury' on this occasion.

You shall Swear by the Custom of our Confession
That you never made any Nuptial Transgression
Since you were marri'd Man & Wife
By Household Brawls or Contentious Strife
Or otherwise in Bed or at Board
Offended each other in Deed or in Word
Or since the Parish Clerk said Amen
Wish'd yourselves unmarri'd agen
Or in a Twelve Month & a day
Repented not in thought any way
But Continued true & in desire
As when you join'd hands in Holy Quire
If to these Conditions without all fear
Of your own Accord you will freely Swear
A Gammon of Bacon you shall receive
And bear it hence with Love & good Leave
For this is our Custom at Dunmow well known
Though the Sport[1] be ours, the Bacon's your own

Upon Which a Gammon of Bacon was delivered to the said Thomas Shakeshaft & Ann his Wife with the usual Solempnity (see *Plate IX*).

The Shakeshaft award evidently created much excitement. After the ceremony, the jury, with the steward of the manor, were invited to dinner with Mr. Thomas Bridge at Great Dunmow ; in the evening, the company adjourned to the ' Saracen's Head ', where with many more ladies and gentlemen, dancing and card playing were enjoyed. A souvenir in the form of a true lovers' knot of bright yellow ribbed silk ribbon, edged with pink, and inscribed in white paint on the bow ' Dunmow Bacon was taken June 20, 1751 ' was worn at the presentation.

A picture (see *Plates X, XI*) of the procession moving away from Little Dunmow was painted by David Ogborne, a London artist, and the father of John who married Elizabeth, daughter of Mrs. Jane Jackson and Sir John Eliot, bt. Elizabeth Ogborne is remembered as one of the historians of Essex and her work, although incomplete, is regarded as a desirable item in any Essex library.

For many years Ogborne has been accepted as the creator of the first pictorial record of the Flitch procession, but this claim must be refuted in the light of researches by Mr. Alfred Hills, F.S.A., and the late Sir Gurney Benham. It appears that among the few examples which have survived of those cotton handkerchiefs printed as souvenirs of popular events, there is one showing a scene similar to that painted by Ogborne. This handkerchief, 2 ft. 5 ins. x 2 ft. 8 ins. bears the signature ' W. Sherwin Sculpt.' at

[1]Both Dugdale and Morant quote ' pleasure ' instead of ' sport '.

C

the bottom right-hand corner (see *Plate VII*) and the oath round the edges. Sherwin, one of the earliest workers in mezzotint, flourished between 1670 and 1710, so it is certain that the scene on the hand-kerchief represents one of the couples during the 1701 festivities, and Ogborne, getting possession of one of these treasured relics, based his picture of the 1751 ceremony upon it.

Comparing the two scenes, one is struck by the similarity in posture of the couples, and the positions of them and their attend-ants in relationship to the church and other buildings ; note also the clerical figure preceding the chair and the gammon held aloft. In Sherwin's picture there are no trees in front of the house, but in both pictures, boys are using the tree on the left as a vantage point. It will be seen that the winners of the bacon wear small ruffs round their necks in both scenes, and although the view has been expressed that the happy couples were arrayed in some special costume, I hardly think the theory is tenable because the ceremonies were, so far as we know, few and far between.

Among the figures which have been identified in Ogborne's painting are the Reverend Mark Gretton who signed the certificate of the proceedings, and Jacob Powell, the fat butcher of Stebbing, who is seen to the left of the picture holding his wig and wiping his forehead. Powell died in 1754 aged thirty-seven years, and is said to have weighed nearly forty stone. The two ladies standing near the butcher were members of the Strutt family.

A short and incorrect account of the Shakeshaft ceremony appeared in the *Gentleman's Magazine,* July 1751. Another notice was in the *London Magazine,* and William Hone gives a long description in his *Everyday Book* (vol. II, 1827) where there is an illustration of the claimants, kneeling on two sharply-pointed stones, and taking the oath in the presence of six bachelors and six maidens who stand in a line in front of the closed doors of the interior of a classical building quite unlike anything in Dunmow. This illustration is obviously copied from a much finer one ' Cut, Printed, and Sold by W. and Cluer Dicey, in St. Mary Aldermary Church-Yard in Bow-Lane, Cheapside. Sold also at their Wholesale Warehouse in Northampton ' (see *Plate XXV*). The background of the scene is undoubtedly the fancy of a London artist familiar with Wren's churches. This rare print is an ambitious and success-ful effort in wood engraving ; two margins of the sheet are devoted to a description of all the previous awards, and ends with Mrs. Shakeshaft's confession that she had but one regret of her marriage,

CHAIRING THE WINNERS

This Engraving by George Cruikshank (1792-1878)
closely resembles the Ogborne picture (see p. 18),
and *Plates X, XI*.

see p. 18

FIGURE 1

and that was, that she had not married sooner. The happy couple made more than £50 by selling slices of the bacon they had won 'to several Gentlemen and Ladies present, who were whimsically merry on the occasion '.

In James Caulfield's *Portraits, Memoirs & Characters of Remarkable Persons* (vol. IV, 1820) is an engraving (see *Fig.* 1) by George Cruickshank of Shakeshaft and his wife in the chair, taken from the Ogborne picture. Only a few figures are drawn in detail, those in the background being merely sketched in ; no buildings or trees are shown. Caulfield, like Hone, supplies accounts of Shakeshaft and of the Wichnor custom.

A charming little nineteenth-century jug in my own collection shows the scene as depicted by Ogborne, but it is stamped on the bottom 'Made in Germany '. The scene, in colour, was also put on plates, candlesticks, etc. sold as souvenirs during the nineteenth century, marked, in large letters, ' A Present from Dunmow '.

*   *   *   *

For the benefit of collectors of old engravings, it may be helpful to mention the three states of Ogborne's work :

1. That which has the signature ' C. Mosely Sculpt. ' in the lower right-hand corner of the plate ' Publish'd according to Act of Parliament Janry. 1752 '.

2. The impression which has the engraver's name immediately under the engraving, and the space it formerly occupied filled with ' Republished, Oct. 28th, 1826 by R. Cribb, 288 Holborn '. The original publication date remains as on the earlier example. An excellent reproduction of this state of the engraving appeared in *The Graphic*, 12 August, 1893.

3. An unsigned lithograph which is the Ogborne picture in reverse, i.e. seen as if the original were reflected in a mirror. This rare state was apparently done by a ' pirate ' who seems to have had a print of the original engraving pasted on to his stone and then traced the outline ; this would give the scene in reverse when impressions were taken off.

CHAPTER V

SOME ASPECTS OF THE EARLY TRIALS

Ah ! madam, cease to be mistaken,
Few married fowl peck Dunmow bacon.
Matthew Prior: *The Dialogue between the Sparrow and Turtle.*

It is clear from the foregoing accounts that although the Shakeshaft ceremony was the last legitimate one, the obligation to provide the bacon, if demanded, was still incumbent upon the lord of the manor, but before we come to examine the debasement of the custom, we must consider a few aspects of the six recorded awards—three under monastic and three under lay lords of the manor.

In the case of the earliest claimants, Wright (1445), Samuel (1467), and Fuller (1510), the awards were made to men only— their wives are not mentioned. To the last two, as in the awards to William and Jane Parsley (1701), John and Ann Reynolds (1701), and Thomas and Ann Shakeshaft (1751), gammons and not flitches of bacon were given ; a gammon is only the thigh of a pig, whereas a flitch is a whole side of the animal. This difference is further emphasised by a receipt given on behalf of Queen Elizabeth's yeo- man purveyor in March, 1586-7, which specifies ' flytches of bacon without gambons ' ; the original document is preserved among the Essex Quarter Sessions Records—a rich hunting-ground for local historians, but unfortunately lacking any direct references to the Dunmow Custom. The term ' bacon-leg ' was found by Miss E. M. Middleton in the parish records of Theydon Garnon, 1719, and is mentioned in her valuable, but as yet unpublished, thesis, ' A Lexicographical Study of Vocabulary Selected from Essex Local Records ', of which a copy is available in the Essex Record Office.

Until 1701 there is no mention of a jury (or manorial homage) being called upon to assess the validity of the claims, and it must be assumed that the seriousness of the oath was sufficient to prevent claimants from committing perjury. On the occasion of the 1701 ceremony, it will be seen that only ladies were asked to serve as a jury, and four of them—Elizabeth, Henrietta, Ann, and Jane Beaumont—were daughters of the lord of the manor, while the fifth—Mary—was the daughter of Thomas Wheeler, the steward. This shows that the first ceremony to be held after the dissolution of the monasteries was in the nature of a revival, with the addition of a ' jury ' to give some semblance of propriety to what was really a jocular manorial court. By 1751, the jury had grown into six bachelors and six spinsters whose judgment was thought to be impartial when the claims of a married couple had to be tested. It is on this 1751 model that all subsequent ceremonies have been based, but with a ' judge ' to take the place of the steward of the manor.

It has been suggested that the words of the oath are of eighteenth century date, but as Fuller, in his *Worthies of England* (1662), and William Winstanley, in *Histories and Observations, Domestick or Foreign; or a Miscellany of Historical Rarities* (1683), quote the oath in substantially the same form as used in 1701, there is little reason to suppose that it is of late composition.

Chambers' *Book of Days* has an account of the Flitch ceremony which says that a claim was made in 1763, but there is no evidence to support it. The *Essex Review* (vol. lii) quotes an extract from Dodsley's *Annual Register* which is worth repeating here :

June 25 (1764).

Mr. and Mrs. Liddal, at the Green Dragon, at Harrowgate [Harrogate, Yorks.], took the flitch of bacon oath at Dunmow in Essex, when the gentlemen of the neighbourhood, to celebrate so unusual an instance of conjugal felicity, sent in each some elegant or plentiful dish, and all dined together in the house of the happy couple.

This feast was apparently held at Harrogate, not at Little Dunmow.

In 1766, however, the *Chelmsford Chronicle* reports that William Shagborough of Bradwell-juxta-Coggeshall, husbandman, and his wife, have claimed the flitch of bacon given ' at the Dunmow Priory, and the procession is to be very speedily ' ; there is nothing to show that the award was ever made to this couple. In this same year died, at Bath, the Earl and Countess of Sutherland, who were so happy that had they recovered from their fatal illnesses, they intended to have claimed the bacon.

CHAPTER VI

PRIVATE AWARDS OF THE FLITCH

El tocino del Paraiso el casado no arrepiso.
[Bacon of paradise for the married who repent not.]

Spanish Proverb.

From a newspaper cutting of 1830 we learn that the Duke of St. Albans said on the anniversary of his marriage :

"We claim then, boldly claim thy flitch, Dunmow,
First of the blest who keep the marriage vow."

But his Grace only obtained a silver representation of the coveted prize, and we do not know how big this was or who was the donor.

An application for the Flitch was made to the steward of the Manor of Little Dunmow Priory by Mr. Joshua Vines, a retired cheesemonger of Reading, and his wife, in 1832. The affair was reported in the *Colchester Gazette* where it is said :

It does not appear, however, that the respectable Steward [Mr. George Wade[1]] feels so warm a desire to renew this, what may be termed jocular, but at the same time, idle custom, which on former occasions was the means of bringing together a large concourse of people, some of whom but of indifferent character, who destroyed the fences in the neighbour-hood, and did considerable mischief in other respects, and without leaving the trace of any substantial benefit as a compensation for the injuries inflicted upon the occupiers in the vicinity.

It is said that Mr. Vines consulted his solicitor as to the best means of enforcing his claim, but there is no record that he was successful.

The *Chelmsford Chronicle* of 30 September 1836 made this announcement :

The Dunmow Flitch. Though the claim for the flitch of bacon was some time since resisted by the ancient authorities at Dunmow, we beg to apprize all devout observers of a long honeymoon that they have

---

[1]His practice, under the style of Wade & Davies, is now in the hands of Mr. J. G. Shergold who acted as Clerk of the Court at the 1949 'Trials'. I am grateful to him for the many items of local historical interest which he has been instrumental in preserving.

now a chance of obtaining it. At the agricultural dinner, on Monday, it will be seen, the Mayor of Saffron Walden offered a flitch, which will be disposed of at the anniversary meeting next year. Oh, ye loving couples, what a chance for immortality !

The prize was duly won, and commemorated on a handbill which is illustrated on *Fig.* 2.

The happy marriage of Queen Victoria and her Consort gave rise to a popular belief that in 1841 the lord of the manor of Little Dunmow privately offered a flitch to Her Majesty ; the compliment was not accepted even if, indeed, it was ever offered. The story evidently grew up around the lithograph (published 11 February 1841, a year and a day after the Queen's marriage) by John Doyle which bore the title :

Stothard's Admired Picture of
" The Procession of the Flitch of Bacon ".
Somewhat Metamorphosed !

and was a caricature based on Thomas Stothard's (1755-1834) important engraving ' The Ceremony of the Dunmow Flitch ', published in 1833 and dedicated to Samuel Rogers, the poet (see *Plate XIV*).

Doyle's picture (*Plate XV*) shows the youthful Queen seated on a white horse behind Prince Albert ; preceding the Royal pair are Lords Duncannon, Morpeth, and Brougham, and Sir Francis Burdett playing musical instruments, then Lord Cottenham—the rotund Lord Chancellor—mounted on a horse and clutching the bacon. Two maidens scatter herbs before the Queen who is followed by Palmerston, Wellington, Melbourne, Lord Normanby, Peel, Lord John Russell, H.R.H. the Duchess of Kent, Sir James Graham, Lord Stanley (later Earl of Derby), William Howley (Archbishop of Canterbury), and the Queen's uncles, T.R.H. the Dukes of Cambridge and Sussex.

This picture is therefore a tribute by all the political parties to the happiness of the royal marriage, and reflects the sentiment of a poem entitled, ' Conversation at Dunmow On the 10th of February, 1840 ', which appeared in the *Essex Herald* :

> " What means the silence of your town ? "
> A gay good-humour'd traveller said,
> " You are so silent and so down
> One would believe the Queen was dead ! "
>
> " Oh ! no, we're saving up our store,
> Knowing the Queen will so bewitch,
> That in a year and one day more
> She will be here to claim the flitch ".

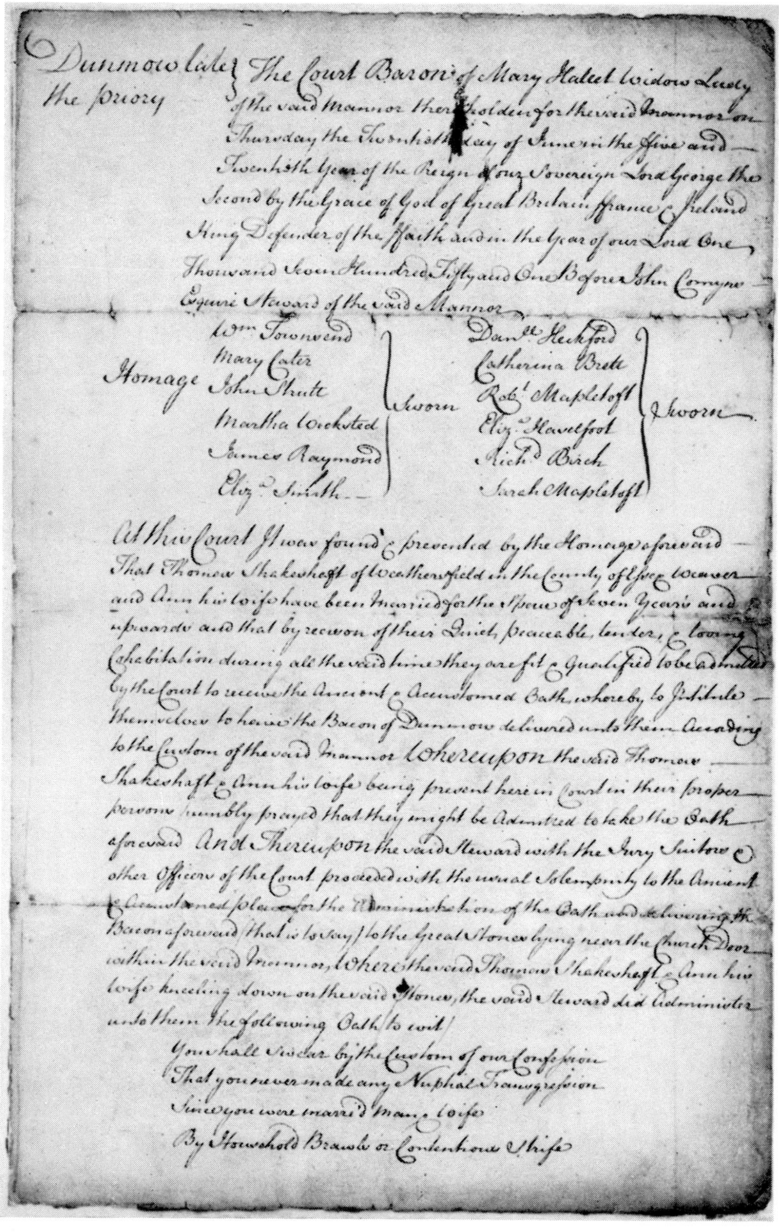

PLATE IX

Dunmow alias The Court Baron of Mary Hallet Widow Lady
the priory of the said Mannor there Holden for the said Mannor on
Thursday the Twentieth day of June in the five and
Twentieth Year of the Reign of our Sovereign Lord George the
Second by the Grace of God of Great Britain France & Ireland
King Defender of the Faith and in the Year of our Lord One
Thousand seven Hundred Fifty and One Before John Comyns
Esqure Steward of the said Mannor

Homage:
Wm Townsend, Mary Cater, John Shute, Martha Wickstead, James Raymond, Elizh Smith — Sworn
Danll Heckford, Catherina Brett, Robt Mapletoft, Elizh Hazelfoot, Richd Birch, Sarah Mapletoft — Sworn

At this Court It was found & presented by the Homage aforesaid
That Thomas Shakeshaft of Weathersfield in the County of Essex Weaver
and Ann his wife have been Married for the Space of Seven Years and
upwards and that by reason of their Quiet, peaceable, tender, & loving
Cohabitation during all the said time they are fit & Qualified to be Admitted
by the Court to receive the Ancient & Accustomed Oath, whereby to Justitute
themselves to have the Bacon of Dunmow delivered unto them According
to the Custom of the said Mannor Whereupon the said Thomas
Shakeshaft & Ann his wife being present here in Court in their proper
persons humbly prayed that they might be Admitted to take the Oath
aforesaid And Thereupon the said Steward with the Jury Suitors &
other Officers of the Court proceeded with the usual Solemnity to the Ancient
& accustomed place for the Administration of the Oath and delivering the
Bacon aforesaid that is to say to the Great Stones lying near the Church Door
within the said Mannor, Where the said Thomas Shakeshaft & Ann his
wife kneeling down on the said Stones, the said Steward did Administer
unto them the following Oath to wit!

You shall swear by the Custom of our Confession
That you never made any Nuptial Transgression
Since you were married Man & Wife
By Household Brawls or Contentious Strife

PART OF THE MANORIAL RECORD OF THE 1751 AWARD

The Court Rolls of the Manor of Little Dunmow, 1458-9, 1530-87, now in
the Essex Record Office, do not contain any references to Awards of the
Bacon.

PLATE X

This painting, for many years in private ownership, was purchased by Great Dunmow Parish Council in 1950. It is believed to be the picture on which the engraving reproduced on the opposite page is based, and the two should be carefully compared.

PLATE XI

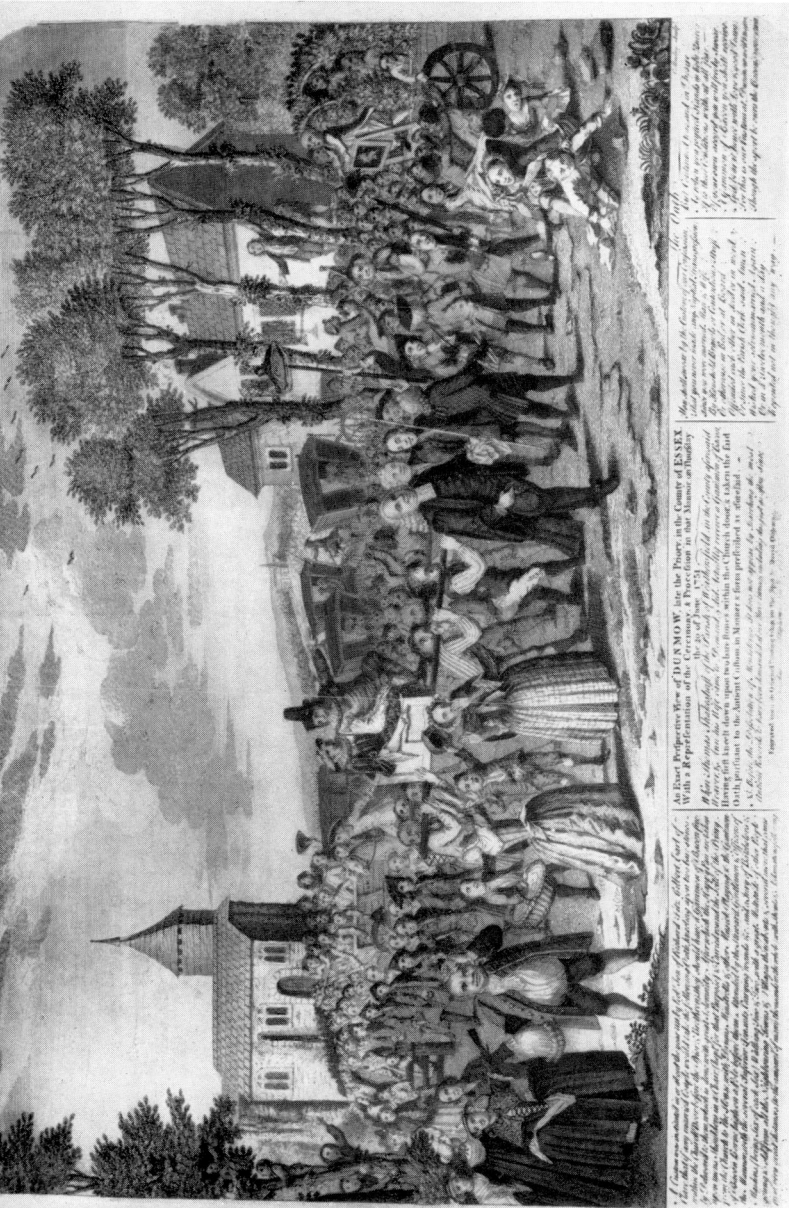

THE PROCESSION OF THOMAS AND ANN SHAKESHAFT AFTER WINNING THE BACON IN 1751

PLATE XII

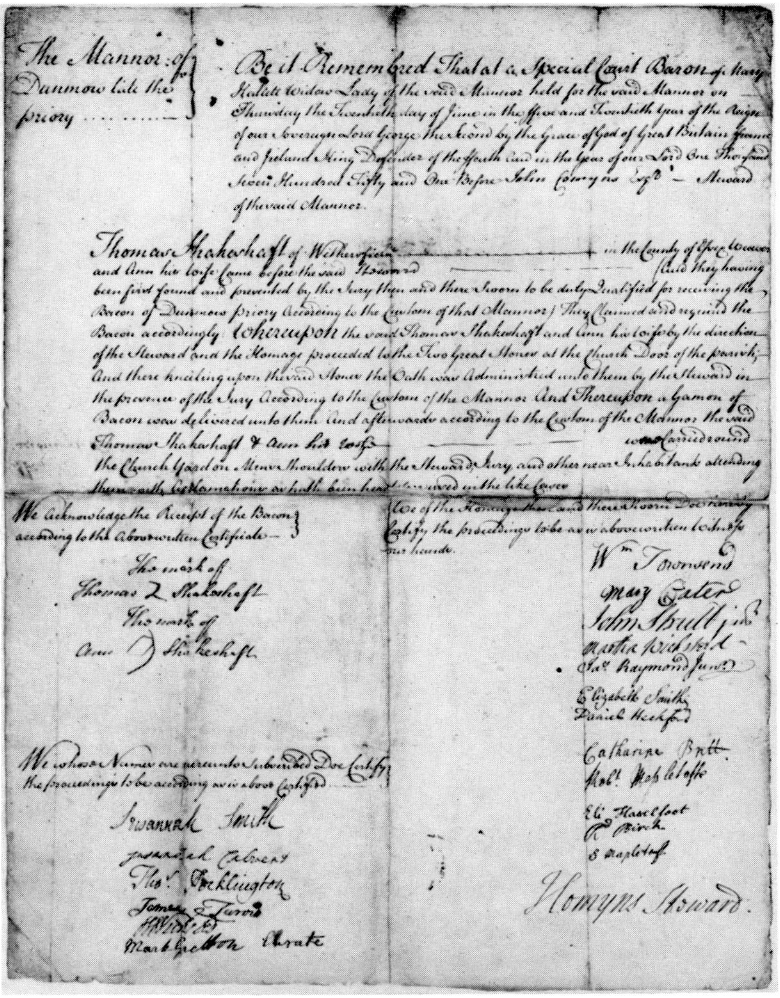

On this document—a record of the 1751 ceremony—is the receipt of
Thomas and Ann Shakeshaft for their Bacon, the signatures of the 'jury',
the Steward, and some of the Witnesses,

John Gilder and his wife Susan, of Terling, made a claim to the bacon on 12 June 1772, and although they appeared with a great concourse of people, they found ' the Priory gates fast nailed in pursuance of the express orders of the Lord of the Manor '. This refusal might well have brought the ancient practice to an end, but folk-memory, especially where ' rights ' are concerned, is long-lived, and the local inhabitants were not accepting a rebuff without a fight.

The Gilder episode passed off, we know not how, but in 1851, just a century after the last award, a Felsted farmer named Hurrell, claimed, and was refused, a gammon of bacon by the lord of the manor. So great was local enthusiasm for the revival of the custom, that the couple were promised a flitch if they attended a fête at Lord Maynard's seat, Easton Lodge. They and some three thousand other people did attend at Little Easton where the bacon was awarded without a ' trial ' amid great rejoicing, band-playing, eating and drinking. Rich and poor, gentle and simple, were obviously anxious that the ancient custom of Dunmow should not be extinguished, but it is with this departure from the manorial aspect of the proceedings that its significance passed away and left only an excuse for merry-making. In modern ' trials ' held in many parts of the country (see Chapter VIII) and abroad, it is the boldness of the claimants rather than conjugal happiness which wins them the bacon.

Thirty-four years after Lord Maynard had made a private award, Lord Northwick made a claim in 1885. This somewhat eccentric peer was then aged 74, and engaged Mr. Stephen Tucker, then Somerset Herald, to correspond with the Rev. J. Hughes-Hallett, lord of the manor of Little Dunmow, and claim the flitch on his behalf. The reverend gentleman finally consented to satisfy his Lordship's ambition by privately presenting him with a flitch ; the coveted prize was then pickled so as to preserve it as an heirloom at Northwick Park, Gloucestershire. Whether or not the preservative chemicals were at fault we have no means of telling, but the bacon was subsequently replaced by a flitch of painted wood and canvas.

After the deaths of all the persons concerned, Mr. Robertson Scott published the correspondence relating to this singular presentation in the *Essex Review,* vol. xxi (1912), pp. 195-205. The lord of the manor, having refused several previous claimants because he thought that the sanctity of the oath was but little regarded, prepared this declaration to accompany his gift to Lord and

D

SAFFRON WALDEN

AND

DUNMOW AGRICULTURAL SOCIETY,

September 25th, 1837.

A Prize of a Gammon of Bacon

WAS PRESENTED TO

Samuel Bloomfield, of Great Dunmow, Labourer in Husbandry, and to Mary, his Wife,

FOR HIGHLY MERITORIOUS CONDUCT,

They having brought up a Family of Nine Children, and placed them in respectable service, without any parochial relief during a union of Forty Years, excepting a time of illness, which continued Seven Weeks.

The Dunmow Flitch was famed in days of yore;
Fitzwalter's gift is offered here no more :
The Priory, and its past account, we leave,
Nor aim its ancient honors to retrieve.
Without exacting oath or compliment,
A Dunmow Gammon still we here present,
To such a pair as well may claim the gift—
Since by their prudent care and household thrift,
And patient conduct which all praise outvies,
They've prov'd to us deserving of this prize.
For many a year they've honorably toiled,—
Paternal feelings have their cares beguiled ;
And now they learn they have not toiled in vain,
While their good name will prove their children's gain.
The hands of industry can never fail ;
Sober and virtuous conduct must avail ;
And on their dying bed, and oft before,
Fond memory will to upright minds restore
A grateful sense of all their by-gone days,
Rendering to man his due, and God the praise.

Hail to this Couple ! friendly greetings give !
Long may they happily as worthy—live !
Long may their sons and daughters far excel
In prudent care, where they have done so well !
An honored lot is theirs !—may many more
Be proud to claim the Bacon we restore !

Bloomfield has (with the intermission of 1 Year and 9 Months) lived in the service of John Fuller, Esq. of Dunmow, and his Predecessor.

HART, PRINTER, WALDEN.

HANDBILL TO COMMEMORATE AN AWARD OF BACON TO A LABOURER AND HIS WIFE, 1837

FIGURE 2

Lady Northwick :

Dunmow, late The Priory,
20th Jan. 1886

WHEREAS George Rushout Baron Northwick and Elizabeth Augusta his wife have made claim to the Bacon of Dunmow, stating they have been married for the space of eleven years past and upwards, and are willing to take the ancient accustomed oath that they have lived all those years in quiet peaceable tender and loving co-habitation

AND WHEREAS the custom of giving a Gammon of Bacon to such claimants has become obsolete and disused in the Manor, and it appears undesirable to renew it : I, James Hughes-Hallett, Lord of the said Manor, being assured that George Rushout Lord Northwick and Elizabeth Augusta his wife could with a safe conscience make the prescribed oath, of my own good will privately present unto them the Bacon, without the usual solemnity, but with the hearty wish that for many years to come they may 'continue true and in desire as when they joined hands in Holy Choire'.

J. Hughes-Hallett.

Lord Northwick was connected with Essex through his ancestor, Sir James Rushout, 1st bart., who was lord of the manor of Maylands in the Liberty of Havering in 1659. The first Lord Northwick married Rebecca, daughter of Humphrey Bowles, of Wanstead, and their second son, adding his mother's maiden name to his own, had the rather unpleasant style of Rev. the Hon. George Rushout-Bowles ; his son George succeeded his uncle John (died 1859) as the third Baron, the winner of the bacon, on whose death in 1887, the family honours became extinct.

CHAPTER VII

THE CEREMONY REVIVED IN 1855 AND 1857

To the popular Victorian novelist, William Harrison Ainsworth, must be attributed the revival of the Flitch custom as we know it today. Articled to a Manchester solicitor in 1821, Ainsworth went to London to finish his legal studies in 1824 ; two years later he entered the publishing business, and remained in it until 1828. The year 1834 saw the first novel, *Rookwood*, from his pen, and from this initial success, his output of thirty-nine books, mostly of an historical nature, were enjoyed by a large public. *The Flitch of Bacon : or, the Custom of Dunmow. A Tale of English Home,* appeared in 1854 ; the story is set in an imaginary inn, 'The Dunmow Flitch ', in Little Dunmow, once the home of Sir Walter Fitz-Walter. Despite its style, the book was well-received, and served to attract notice to the Essex village. The novel was dramatised by W. Shirley P. Grant in the early years of the present century as a romantic opera under the title *The Dunmow Flitch ; or The Rival Claimants*, and the music was composed by H. F. Henniker, Mus.Doc.

It would perhaps be more correct to say that attention was drawn to Great, rather than to Little, Dunmow, for it was in the larger parish that a Committee was formed to revive the Flitch ceremony which was first held, shorn of any manorial associations, in the Town Hall, on Thursday, 19th July, 1855.

Accounts in periodicals and newspapers of the day provide us with the background to the festivities on which no expense was spared. No sooner had notice been given in the local press that a flitch ' trial ' was to be held, than claims ' as numerous as the leaves on a rose, and each one as full as a Dutch woman's skirt ' were received by the Committee ; a reproduction of one of the original notices is shown opposite (*Fig.* 3).

The great day arrived. At 7 a.m. it was raining in London,

THE DUNMOW FLITCH.

NOTICE IS HEREBY GIVEN,

That all Claimants for the FLITCH of BACON, to be presented at Dunmow, in July, 1855, by WM. HARRISON AINSWORTH, Esq., must forward their applications before the 24th June next, and attend personally at the TOWN HALL, DUNMOW, to prove their title to the prize in open Court. Such Claimants and their Witnesses will be examined before a Jury of Maidens and Bachelors; and will be required to take the Oath according to old custom. The successful Candidates will be afterwards carried in procession to a Fête to be held near the Town.

The Committee have to urge on Claimants, that the prize must not be estimated by its cost, but by the distinction it offers to those who may be fortunate enough to obtain it. Enviable are the wedded pair on whom the prize is conferred, since the acquisition establishes a claim to honor and respect. To say that a couple "deserve the Flitch" is a high Compliment,—to say that "they have actually won it," is to proclaim them amongst the best and happiest of mankind.

BY ORDER OF THE COMMITTEE,

CHARLES PAVEY.

———

Applicants for the Flitch can receive the form of Oath, and all particulars, by forwarding two postage Stamps to MR. C. PAVEY, Dunmow, Essex.

WILLIAM HARRISON AINSWORTH REVIVES THE FLITCH CEREMONY IN 1855

A reduced copy of one of the original Notices

FIGURE 3

but that did not prevent a large number of people travelling by special trains to Bishop's Stortford where they were met by carts, waggons, vans, and any other vehicle capable of carrying passengers to Dunmow ; these conveyances were decorated with flowers and branches of trees. Men with trucks of strawberries and barrows of oysters were hurrying to the fairgound ; all the shops were shut, and bonnets were thrust out of every window of the 'Saracen's Head' so eager were their owners to watch the arrival of spectators. Men on the roofs of houses in front of the Town Hall were getting wet through, but nothing could deter the enthusiasm of the crowds ; a large number of the local inhabitants were dressed in green smock-frocks with highly embroidered shoulders and breast-pieces. Most of the public-houses were filled, and as many parties had arrived the previous evening, lodgings were fully occupied and any form of shelter was at a premium. Many of the clergy in the district opposed the revival of the custom, and feeling ran so high that hostile papers were distributed in the neighbourhood and an acrimonious correspondence appeared in the county papers. Whatever the gentry might have felt, it was evident that this excuse for jollification was very popular among the Dunmow people.

Mr. E. T. Smith, lessee of the Drury Lane Theatre, was responsible for the provision of banners, garlands, costumes, and other decorations. The interior of the Town Hall, a very small area with a little gallery on one side, was ornamented with the flitches suspended from blue frames with wreaths of artificial flowers twined round them. Flower baskets and wands decorated the green baize 'jury' box which was to accommodate the six bachelors in their best clothes, with their hair greased 'with great liberality and ostentation, due care being bestowed on the curl that rested—round as an eyeglass—in the centre of the forehead'. The reporter of the *Illustrated Times* dismisses the bachelors in a few lines, but not so their companions, the spinsters, who are treated in this melodramatic style of journalism :

'But the virgins ! It would take a volume to describe them properly —their eyes alone would require an entire chapter, and numerous coloured illustrations. Three of the virgins had light hair, varying in tint from a bright amber [this was Lydia Collis] to a deep rich Margate slipper [Emily Richardson]. They wore their hair brushed back from the forehead, with the loose twisting curls gathered together in a round cushion that encircled the head like a glory of gold. Their eyelids were delicate and transparent as rose leaves, their mouths were only just large enough for mince meat to pass through, and to this day, it appears to us a miracle how they managed to breathe down their wonderfully minute noses. The other three young ladies were *brunettes.*'

The court-room was mostly occupied by ladies whose ' tiers of pretty faces, and eyes brighter than jewels on the court dress of a duchess ' made such an appeal to a writer in *The Lady's Newspaper and Pictorial Times*. The proceedings opened at two o'clock with the rain beating like small shot against the bay window of the room. An entrance fee of five shillings was charged for the privilege of being a spectator and hearing Mr. Harrison Ainsworth, who presided, give an account of the history of the custom. Mr. Charles Pavey, of Dunmow, was the clerk of the court, Mr. Robert Bell was counsel for the claimants, while Mr. Dudley Costello appeared in a similar role on behalf of the donors of the bacon.

Two couples had been selected from the many applicants anxious to prove their claim. They were James and Hannah Barlow, of Chipping Ongar, and M. Jean Baptiste François Ernest and Madame Clara de Chatelain, of London ; the latter couple had applied for the flitch in 1845 when the lord of the manor informed them that the custom had fallen into desuetude. Witnesses attested to the happiness of the couples who were awarded flitches amidst applause and laughter.

After the examinations, the sun shone in full force, and a procession to the Windmill Field was formed in the following order :

Marshal
Stud of horses, mounted by yeomen in appropriate dresses, carrying banners, with the names of all the claimants since the 13th century inscribed on them and the names of persons associated with the custom.
Ladies with garlands.
Banners borne by rustics.
Maidens and bachelors of the jury in a carriage.
The Clerk and the Crier of the Court, and Counsel in a carriage.
Other officers of the court.
Gentlemen with wands.
Flitch of bacon carried by four yeomen.
Band.
Mr. & Mrs. Barlow carried on a chair on men's shoulders.
Gentlemen with wands.
Banners borne by rustics.
Two minstrels playing pipe and tabor.
Flitch of bacon carried by four yeomen.
Band.
Le Chevalier and Madame de Chatelain carried on a chair.
Mr. Harrison Ainsworth in a carriage.

Reports are at variance about the exact order of the procession. and the taking of the oath. Some accounts say that during its course through the principal streets of the town (see *Plates XVIII, XIX*), the procession halted at the market cross (formerly opposite the Town Hall), proclamation made by the sound of drum and trumpet of the awards, and the flitches delivered to the claimants in a field not far off. The *Chelmsford Chronicle* says that the stones specially made for the occasion (without the traditional sharp points, and inscribed ' Remember your oath ') could not be made available ' whether from their weight or some whim of the stony-hearted mason was not explained, so it was decided to dispense with stones, oath and all '. The flitches weighed ninety and eighty-eight pounds respectively, and were from a pig bred by Mr. Livermore, of Langleys Farm, Great Dunmow, and cured by Mr. Taylor of Dunmow ; one was presented by Mr. Ainsworth, and from the following letter to Joseph Clarke of Saffron Walden it would seem that he had intended the fact to be well publicised :

> 5, Arundel Terrace,
> Kemp Town, Brighton.
> June 22, 1855.
>
> My Dear Sir,
>
> I have received Mr. Smith's posting bill.
>
> It is well enough ; but he ought to have stated that the Flitch will be given away by me. This is a strange omission, and must be rectified, and I hope you will not put up the bills till it is so. He must send you others. I have written to him on the subject ; but you had better, also, write to him.
>
> The day ought to be fixed. I enclose you a letter from another enquirer, and will thank you to send him information when the point is settled.
>
> Certainly, the print of the procession might be improved—and ought to represent in some measure the proposed ceremony.
>
> Yours faithfully,
> W. HARRISON AINSWORTH.

It was estimated that seven thousand people were present at the fair ground, and while many of these no doubt indulged in the rural sports and other amusements which followed the Flitch ceremony, Mr. Ainsworth presided at a gathering of thirty gentlemen who dined at the ' Saracen's Head ' off a haunch of venison presented by the Viscountess Maynard.

Some derogatory remarks were made in the press about the revival of the custom and about the organisers, one correspondent going so far as to say that the poor will be corrupted by the low, cheap exhibitions, and every other device which the selfish nature of man can concoct to obtain his neighbours hard-earned money. *The Leader* of 21 July 1855 had printed a condemnation of the ceremony and adverse reviews of Ainsworth's *Ballads : Romantic, Fantastical, and Humourous,* and *The Flitch of Bacon.*

In a letter dated 5th August 1856 from Charles Pavey to Joseph Clarke, the writer refers to the circus-like performance put on by Mr. E. T. Smith which did not give entire satisfaction. Pavey suggested that as the novelty was over, only two shillings and six pence should be charged for admission to the court ; he said that Ainsworth had offered another flitch to be competed for in the summer of 1857, and five pounds towards the general expenses. *The Times,* 18th November 1856, contained this announcement :

Important to all about to Marry

A generous and soft-hearted lady, whose name at present is with great judgment not disclosed, has intimated to the proper authorities her intention to invest in the name of the corporation of Great Dunmow a sufficient sum to perpetuate the ancient custom of Dunmow (as revived by Mr. H. Ainsworth), the interest being sufficient to discharge the expenses attendant on the annual ceremony at the town hall and procession. The successful claimants, instead of taking the old and almost impracticable oath formerly required, will declare that " they have lived together a twelvemonth and a day without any quarrel or any wish to be unmarried again ", and will then receive the prize.

This offer did not materialise, and although no award was made in 1856, Great Dunmow was again *en fête* on 25th June 1857 (see *Fig.* 4). Triumphal arches at the entrances to the town from Chelmsford, Thaxted and London, with the word ' Welcome ' on one side, and a loyal motto on the reverse, had been erected, bands from Saffron Walden and Bocking were in attendance, and there was a battery of sixteen cannon which fired at 6 a.m. and at intervals during the day.

Mr. Ainsworth presided at the ' trials ' of two claimants, but as there was only one flitch, the jury awarded it to Mr. and Mrs. Thomas Jeremiah Heard, of Bentley, Staffordshire, and a pair of silver sugar tongs was given to the other competitors as a consolation prize. The proceedings were similar to those held in 1855, archery and other sports being an attraction for a large crowd of people at the conclusion of the ceremony.

A Dunmow Flitch Guarantee Fund had been formed with a capital of £40 in shares of five shillings each in order to provide music, banners and amusements, and to pay for printing and advertising ' so that the Festival may be carried out in a respectable and handsome manner according to the plan approved of by W. H. Ainsworth, Esq. '. After the 1857 ceremony, a report of the Committee was sent to shareholders and subscribers, and one cannot forbear to mention that the Committee congratulated themselves ' on the successful issue of their undertaking, which, it is hoped,

E

DUNMOW FLITCH OF BACON

PRESENTED BY W. H. AINSWORTH, ESQ.,
25TH JUNE, 1857.

CLAIMANTS FOR THE BACON

WILLIAM SPARKE, AND RUTH PAVELY, HIS WIFE.
THOMAS J. HEARD, AND SARAH, HIS WIFE.
JEREMY O'BRIEN, AND MARGARET, HIS WIFE.

At 10 o'Clock the several Claimants will enter the Town, escorted by Bands of Music.

AT 1 O'CLOCK, P. M., THE COURT WILL OPEN AT THE TOWN HALL

The Jury of Maidens and Bachelors will be selected, the Claimants and their Witnesses examined by Counsel, and the Jury, under the direction of the President, will decide which Couple shall receive the prize.

The Court will then adjourn to an adjoining Meadow, in Procession, and the Flitch of Bacon will be there presented to the happy Couple, on their making the usual solemn declaration, kneeling on two Stones. The unsuccessful Claimants will each receive a silver ornament as a memento of the occasion.

ORDER OF PROCESSION.

MARSHAL, ON HORSEBACK, TWO BANDS OF MUSIC, WITH FLAGS AND MOTTOES,

Banners, with the names of the successful Claimants from the year 1445, to the present time, Coats of Arms of the founder of the Custom, and of those who assisted in its revival, Arms of the principal Land Owners in Dunmow, and the Vicinity,

THE FLITCH OF BACON, SUSPENDED ON FOUR POLES

GARLANDS, AND DEVICES IN FLOWERS,

THE HAPPY COUPLE IN A CHAIR, BORNE BY EIGHT MEN

JURY OF MAIDENS AND BACHELORS, in an open Carriage, drawn by Four Horses,
CARRIAGE CONTAINING THE UNSUCCESSFUL CANDIDATES AND THE WITNESSES.
CARRIAGE CONTAINING THE OFFICERS OF THE COURT.

RURAL SPORTS.

Country Dances; Gingling Match; Foot Race; Hurdle Race; Sack Race; Wheelbarrow Race; Sports for Juveniles, and Climbing a lofty Pole for a prize.

The Town will be decorated with Flags; several Triumphal Arches will be placed across the Highway; a Battery of Toy Cannon will be erected in the Meadow, and discharged at intervals in the Afternoon.

Tickets of Admission to the Town Hall, 2s. 6d. each, to be had at the doors, and of Mr. Carter, Bookseller, Dunmow,—to the Meadow 1s. each, for the first two hours, then 6d. Children Halfprice.

A PRINT of the TOWN HALL has been published by MR. BARFIELD, Dunmow. Price 1s...6d. Proofs 2s. Colored 3s. Post Free.

Programmes of the Procession with full particulars of the ancient Custom are published in a Pamphlet, and may be had of Mr. Pavey, the Secretary to the Committee, High-Street Dunmow. Post Free for Seven Stamps.

Arrangements have been made with the Eastern Counties Railway Company, for conveying passengers on that day between London and Bishop Stortford, and Cambridge and Bishop Stortford, and between Colchester and Braintree, and the intermediate Stations at a Single Fare.

TRAINS—London to Stortford, 1st, 2nd, & 3rd, 6. 27. a. m., 1st, & 2nd, 8 a. m., and 10. 57. a. m.—Returning to London, 1st, 2nd, & 3rd, 8. 14. p. m. From Cambridge, 1st, & 2nd, 7. a. m., 1st, 2nd, & 3rd, 9. 40. a. m.,—Returning to Cambridge, 1st, 2nd, and 3rd, 5. 24. p. m., and 10. 12. p. m. From Colchester to Braintree, 1st, 2nd, and 3rd, 8. 57. a. m.—Returning to Colchester, 1st, 2nd, and 3rd, 6. 40. p. m.

Further Particulars afforded, and every facility given by MR. PATMORE, Railway Inn, Bishop Stortford, who will provide Carriages and Conveyances to meet the Trains arrival, and other parties will convey Passengers to and from the Trains between Braintree and Dunmow.

CARTER, PRINTER, AND STATIONER, HIGH-STREET DUNMOW

PROGRAMME OF THE 1857 CELEBRATIONS

FIGURE 4

has given pleasure to all and offence to none ; for, as it was observed in one of the local papers, there was nothing to be seen to
offend the most fastidious, or to cause the most decorous persons
to regret their attendance as spectators '.

The thanks of the organisers were accorded to Ainsworth
and the counsel, to Joseph Clarke of Saffron Walden for banners,
flags, and other decorations, to Mr. H. E. Cockayne for flags,
spears and battleaxes, to J. Maryon Wilson for ropes, posts, and
his cannon, to the Chief Constable and the local Superintendent,
and all the other helpers who are listed in detail.

CHAPTER VIII

NOTES OF 'TRIALS' HELD BETWEEN 1855 AND 1949

The following pages are devoted to particulars, in tabulated form and as complete as possible, of such awards as have been made since the custom ceased to have any manorial significance. Local newspapers and souvenir programmes have been the main sources of information, and it will be seen throughout that the ceremony had degenerated from its former solemnity into little more than an excuse for jollification. The judge, jury, and counsel, and other officers of the 'court' are a purely modern innovation, and merely a travesty of the ancient manorial court held by the steward of the manor assisted by a 'homage' or select body of jurymen or assessors.

Harrison Ainsworth little thought that his revival of almost a century ago would have had such far-reaching effects and maintained such continuous interest. That an out-of-the-way Essex village should be responsible for the perpetuation of a custom which has been repeated in many places (including America) in a variety of guises, and finally becomes a subject for television, shows the love of the average Englishman for tradition. The lists which follow are a tribute to those couples who have been bold enough to face a gruelling, even if facetious, public cross-examination concerning their married lives for the entertainment of their fellows.

19 July 1855[1]

Held at Town Hall, Great Dunmow.
Judge—William Harrison Ainsworth (see *Plate XIII*).
Jury—Lydia Collis, Emily Richardson, Emma Hunter, Jane Tressidy, Sarah Johnson, Emma Halliday.
Philip Johnson, Frederick Giblin, William Franklin, Charles Prior, Henry Pinkney, Joseph Coates.
Counsel for claimants—Robert Bell.
Counsel for the bacon—Dudley Costello.
Crier of the court—Charles Pavey.

[1]See pp. 26-30.

Claimants—James Barlow, bricklayer and builder, between 40 and 50 years of age, and his wife Hannah, of Chipping Ongar.
 Jean Baptiste François Ernest de Chatelain, and his wife Clara, of London.
Weather—Wet at first, but fine in afternoon.
Attendance—Estimated at 7,000.
Organizer—E. T. Smith, lessee of Drury Lane Theatre.
Authorities—*Essex Herald*, 17 July 1855 ; *The Leader*, 21 July 1855 ; *Chelmsford Chronicle*, 27 July 1855 ; *Illustrated Times, The Lady's Newspaper and Pictorial Times, Illustrated London News*, all of 28 July 1855 ; *Bentley's Miscellany*, vol. xxxviii.

25 June 1857

Held at Town Hall, Great Dunmow.
Judge—William Harrison Ainsworth.
Jury—Misses Bell, Joyce, E. Abbott, Abbott, Newman, Sweeting.
 Messrs. Morton, Franklin, Coates, Parris, Childs, Tylor.
Counsel for the claimants—John Baron Bowker.
Counsel for the bacon—Dudley Costello.
Crier of the court—James Barlow, who had won the bacon in 1855.

Men if you would live happy lives,
 Adore, protect and love your wives,
Cherish them by day and night,
 Never quarrel, scold or fight . . .

HEADING OF A BROADSHEET ISSUED IN 1857

FIGURE 5

Claimants—Thomas Jeremiah Heard, police officer, aged 35, and his wife
 Sarah, of Bentley, Staffordshire.
 John Nichol Hawkins, M.D., and his wife Ann Sophia, of Victoria
 Place, Regent's Park, London.
Weather—Favourable.
Organizer—Charles Pavey, of Great Dunmow.

Notes—Heard's brother was at one time bailiff at Bassingbourne
 Hall, Hatfield Broad Oak, and his father lived near Takeley.
 Dr. Hawkins was described as grave and sedate with a tinge
 of white on his whiskers, and had been married about two
 years. Bacon was given by Harrison Ainsworth and E. T.
 Smith (see also p. 31).

Authority—*Essex Herald,* 30 June 1857.

16 August 1869

Held in a marquee.
Judge—E. T. Smith, who had organized the 1855 ceremony.
Jury—Mary Ann Childs, Julia Murphy, Catherine Childs, Patience Darwin,
 Margaret Mason, Maria Bedlow.
 Peter Murphy, Walter White, William Butcher, Walter Thomas Bates,
 Charles Mackenzie, Alfred Edward Agar.
Counsel for the claimants—E. Garden, of the Lyceum Theatre, London.
Counsel for the bacon—H. G. Brookes.
Clerk of the court—Charles Pavey.
Crier of the court—Mr. Terry.
Claimants—William Casson, wood engraver, and his wife Emma Elizabeth,
 of 3 Cornwall Road, Victoria Park, London.
 Josiah Leaver, jeweller, and his wife Mary, of Rydon Crescent,
 Clerkenwell, London.
Weather—Inclined to be cloudy.
Attendance—Reports give figures between 10,000 and 20,000.
Organizer—J. W. Savill, of Great Dunmow.

Notes—There were eighteen applications for the bacon which was
 presented by Fitch & Son, 69 Bishopsgate, London. H. B.
 Sheridan, M.P., was to have been judge, but was prevented
 from attending because one of his daughters was ill. Proceedings opened with a mock cricket match played between
 clowns and the gentlemen of the Dunmow Club. After the
 procession there was a *fête champêtre,* mock tournament,
 bicycle race, music by bands of First Herts. Light Horse and
 Saffron Walden Volunteer Corps, Punch and Judy Show,
 maypole dance, firework display, and other attractions. In
 1858, the Rev. and Mrs. Sophia Lavina Good were accepted
 as claimants for a flitch to be presented in 1859, but no
 trial was held that year. From a newspaper account of 1874,
 we learn that Mrs. Leaver was very annoyed at the unex-
 pected notoriety as a result of the 'trial'. The Dunmow
 Flitch was introduced in a pantomime at the Alexandra
 Palace a few years after the 1869 ceremony.

"**Our Custom of Dunmow.**"

By wisdom given, by custom consecrate,
By genius dowered, by Love and peace endeared,
The Ancient Flitch becomes a trophy great
Of rarest happiness, beloved, revered.

THE ANCIENT CUSTOM OF THE FLITCH OF BACON

INSTITUTED BY

SIR ROBERT FITZWALTER,

AT

St. Mary's Priory, **Little Dunmow,**

ESSEX, (TEMP. HENRY III.,) WILL BE REVIVED AT

THE TOWN HALL, DUNMOW,

On MONDAY, JULY 23rd, 1877,

(" These Celebrations, redolent of good old manners and simplicities, are becoming only too rare among us."
THE ECHO, *May 23rd, 1877.*)

Under the Special Patronage of

W. HARRISON AINSWORTH, ESQ.

Author of "The Flitch of Bacon"

PRESIDENT :— J. W. SAVILL, F.R.H.S.

(OF DUNMOW,)

ADVOCATE :— WILLIAM TEGG, ESQ., F.R.H.S.

Not this a flag from bloody fields well borne,
Nor shield in which a conquered foeman fell,
But the bright badge of Love that knows no morn,
Nor noon, nor night, if truth and trust proved well !

They only win this proudest prize of Love,
Whose true affection trials never shake—
Whose trust on purest Love time's power above
Rests surely, loving on for Love's sweet sake!

A REDUCED COPY OF THE POSTER ADVERTISING THE 1877 CEREMONY

FIGURE 6

Authorities—Hertfordshire Mercury, 17 July 1858 ; *Chelmsford Chronicle,* 20 August 1869 ; W. Andrews : *History of the Dunmow Flitch of Bacon Custom* (1877) ; *The Penny Illustrated Paper,* 24 July 1869.

10 August 1874

Held in a marquee near the British Schools, Great Dunmow.

Judge—William Casson, winner of the bacon in 1869.

Jury—Alice Mary Ann Dowsett, Jane Burton, Elizabeth Kingston, Julia Poole, Ada Sutton, Jane Eve.

William Speller, Frederick Barnard, Charles Julius Butcher, James Norman, William Harrington, George Fisher.

Counsel for the claimants did not appear.

Counsel for the bacon—J. W. Savill.

Claimants—Joseph James Clegg, aged 38, and his wife Hannah, aged 34, c/o The Standard Measure Wine Company, Bury Street Warehouses, St. Mary Axe, London.

Attendance—About 200 in the marquee.

Organizer—Local Court of Foresters (Court Prince Arthur), J. W. Savill, corresponding secretary.

Notes—Claimants did not arrive until about 6 p.m. Admission to the marquee, 2s. 6d. reserved seats ; 1s. 6d. front seats ; 1s. standing. Harrison Ainsworth sent a guinea towards the funds. Band of the West Essex Militia, and the Dunmow drum and fife band under Mr. Willis in attendance. This was one of the worst organized ' trials ' ever staged, but not so bad as that of 1880.

Authority—Chelmsford Chronicle, 14 August 1874.

17 July 1876

Held in marquee on Windmill Field, Dunmow Downs.

Judge—William Andrews, of Hull.

Jury—Alice Newman, Lydia James, Annie P. Savill, Frances Clark, Mary Moore [note only five maidens].

Walter Dowsett, William Mead, Edward Dowsett, George Stokes, Henry Cant, Thomas Hughes.

Counsel for the bacon and crier of the court—J. W. Savill.

Claimants—James Henry Boosey, church clerk and verger, aged 34, and his wife Mary, aged 36, of 1 Springfield Terrace, Ventnor, Isle of Wight.

Attendance—Between 2,000 and 3,000.

Organizer—J. W. Savill.

Notes—Boosey appeared in the uniform of the 5th Isle of Wight Rifle Volunteers. The Rev. Samuel Marriott Smith, vicar of Harwell, Berks., and his wife Caroline, were also chosen as claimants, but did not appear. Bacon presented by Fitch & Son, of London. Usual amusements (including the band of the West Essex Militia) of a country fête were provided. Admission receipts amounted to £87 5s. 10d.

Authority—Chelmsford Chronicle, 21 July 1876.

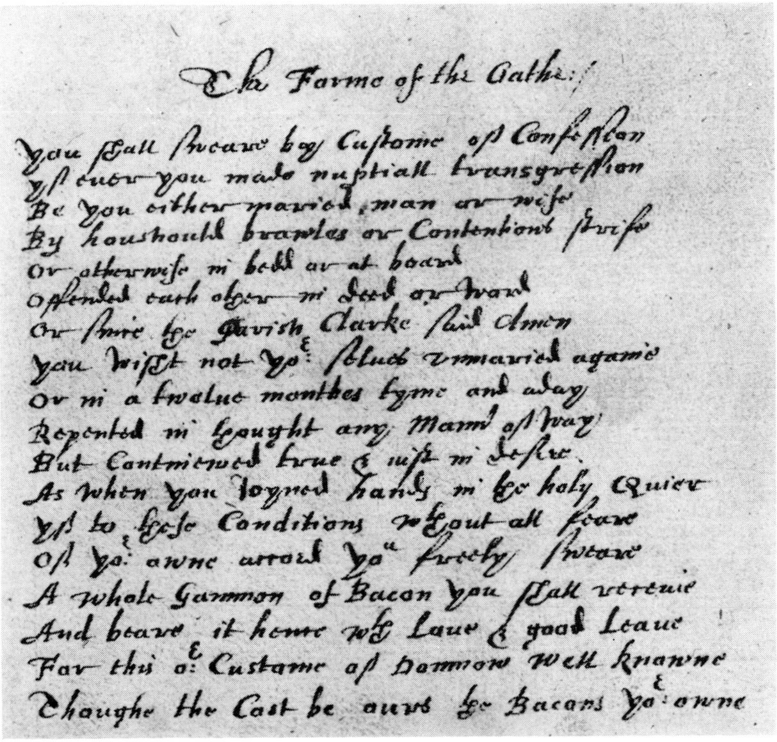

PLATE XVII

The Forme of the Oathe:

You shall sweare by Custome of Confession
Yf euer you made nuptiall transgression
Be you either married man or wife
By houshould brawles or Contentious strife
Or otherwise in bedd or at board
Offended each other in deed or word
Or since the Parish Clarke said Amen
You wisst not yo.r selues vnmaried agayne
Or in a twelue monthes tyme and a day
Repented in thought any Mann' of way
But Contniewed true & iust in desier.
As when you Ioyned hands in th'holy, Quier
Yf to these Conditions w.thout all feare
Of yo.r owne accord yo.u freely sweare
A whole Gammon of Bacon you shall receiue
And beare it home w.th Laue & good Leaue
For this o.r Custome of Dammow well knowne
Thoughe the Cost be ours y.e Bacons yo.r owne

The Form of the Oath as it appears in a Manuscript at the British Museum [Harl.1177]. This should be compared with the version on p. 15.

PLATE XVIII

THE 1855 PROCESSION PASSING GREAT DUNMOW TOWN HALL

PLATE XIX

ANOTHER VIEW OF THE 1855 PROCESSION

PLATE XX

PRIORY PLACE, LITTLE DUNMOW

Built in the first half of the seventeenth century, this picturesque property stands to the west of the Church.

TWO FIFTEENTH-CENTURY COTTAGES

Originally one house, these cottages are a medley of plasterwork, weatherboarding and thatch ; they stand to the north of the Priory Church, Little Dunmow.

23 July 1877

Held at Town Hall, Great Dunmow.
Judge—J. W. Savill, of Great Dunmow.
Jury—Misses Moore, Savill, Farrell, Burge, Cheek, Dowsett.
  Messrs. Plester, Robson, Walker, Woolston, Lilley, Perry.
Counsel for the claimants—William Tegg, a London publisher.
Claimants—James Barrick, foreman bricklayer, aged 49, and his wife
  Hannah, aged 48, of Dunmow.
Weather—Fair at first, but torrential rain and thunderstorm in late after-
  noon.
Attendance—2727 at the fête, and about 50 at the ball held at the Town
  Hall in the evening.
Organizer—J. W. Savill.

Notes—Proceedings opened with a pianoforte recital and songs
    (see p. 71) about which one newspaper said some were more
    anti-Russian than was suitable in a mixed assembly, and
    another suggested that Mr. Gladstone would not have ap-
    proved. Reserved seats 2s. 6d. ; front seats, 2s. ; body of the
    hall, 1s. 6d. ; gallery, 1s. and 6d. Barrick and his wife de-
    scribed as being dressed in sombre black and looking as
    unsentimental as could be imagined ; they had been married
    twenty-eight years and had had twelve children. William
    Andrews (judge for the 1876 'trial') and his wife put in a
    claim, but were prevented from attending because of the
    birth of a child. Another couple, John and Emily Haltridge,
    of Lincoln, arrived at Dunmow, but did not care to face the
    ordeal of a public examination and returned home in disgust ;
    a lot of correspondence—that from Haltridge might be termed
    abusive—appeared in the county newspapers about the cere-
    mony and the intentions of its organizer. Savill, a local
    bookseller and antiquary, said to be a very grave gentleman
    attired in a scarlet smoking cap. Streets decorated with bunt-
    ing, laudatory banners, flags, garlands, heart-shaped cards
    inscribed 'Love, joy, and prosperity'. Procession, headed
    by band of 6th Herts. Rifle Volunteer Corps, to a field near
    the British School where there was a fair with merry-go-
    rounds, side-shows, nigger minstrels, acrobats, eastern fakirs,
    a balloon ascent, and 'shadow pantomime'. One observer
    described the proceedings as an anachronistic farce, and a
    number of London papers criticised the celebrations rather
    unfavourably. *The London Reader* of 18 August 1877 re-
    ported the outburst of a rustic in the gallery during the
    'trial' of James Barrick : 'Oi say Jem, doan't 'ee oie the
    beacon so badly'. The Great Eastern Railway ran excursion
    trains at single fares for the return journey. Admission

receipts, £88 0s. 10d. Bacon presented by Fitch & Son, of Bishopsgate, London.

Authorities—*The Morning Advertiser,* 25 July 1877 ; *Chelmsford Chronicle,* 27 July 1877 ; *Hand & Heart,* 3 August 1877 ; *Newcastle Chronicle,* 4 August 1877 ; *The Sketch,* 1 August 1894 ; *Essex Weekly News,* 14 October 1949.

26 July 1880

Held at Town Hall, Great Dunmow.
Claimants—Joseph Thorne, house decorator, aged 35, and his wife Sarah (née Hedges), aged 34, of St. Andrew Street, Bethnal Green, London.
Weather—Wet, with severe thunderstorm in afternoon, but fine in the evening.
Attendance—Poor.
Organizers—Mr. Friend, of the Alexandra Palace, and J. W. Savill, of Great Dunmow.

Notes—This ' trial ' was farcical. In an account in the *Chelmsford Chronicle,* the unnamed judge is described as deaf, and wearing a high stove-pipe hat, and a dingy white waistcoat and cravat. Thorne was born at Dunmow, and his wife at Braintree ; both wore large gold ear-rings. The judge quibbled about awarding the flitch (given by Fitch & Son, of Bishopsgate, London), but as the claimant was forceful in his demands, a visitor (Mr. Holland, of the North Woolwich Gardens) offered to give him one. The procession and gymnastic performances were dispensed with ; many theatrical properties, including a piebald woman from America, and a tiger and monkey exhibition, were brought from London. There were steam circuses (probably roundabouts), shooting galleries, a greasy pole, and the Braintree Brass Band to entertain the visitors—many of whom were drunk. Admission to the ' trial ' was 2s. 6d. ; the local expenses amounted to £55 5s. 6d. exclusive of new properties, printing, etc., so that the promoters' loss must have exceeded £100. An editorial comment in the *Chelmsford Chronicle* describes the custom as played out and a coarse burlesque. ' The people of Dunmow, and the people of Essex, look upon it now as a low and degrading farce, and it is a matter of regret and shame to them that these periodical efforts should be made to galvanise the thing into life . . . . . The " Custom of Dunmow " will hardly survive the ignominious failure of 1880. If it is sought still to keep it up, we shall not be sorry to see the floods descend again on the day fixed for the exhibition.'

Authority—*Chelmsford Chronicle,* 30 July, 1 October 1880.

'THE FEAST OF THE FLITCH; OR DOINGS AT DUNMOW BY OUR PROPHETIC OLD DUN-MOWRE'

A Cartoon of 1877 from "Funny Folks".

FIGURE 7

4 August 1890

Held in a marquee in the grounds of Newton Hall, Great Dunmow.
Judge—F. W. Bartley.
Jury—Misses Lockyer, Maud Hamilton, Grace Staines, Jenkins, Bird, Monkham.
Henry Gillham, Charles Gillham, Charles Cook, Austin Staines, R. Russell, W. Hamilton.
Counsel for the claimants—Robert Marsh, of Little Canfield.
Counsel for the bacon—R. W. Russell.
Clerk of the court—J. Hamilton, of Great Dunmow.
Claimants—John Hoy, employed by Wood & Son, horticulturalists, of Wood Green, Middlesex, and his wife, of Tottenham.
Attendance—Said to be large.
Organizers—Local Sports Committee.
Notes—Nine applicants of which two were chosen, but only one couple attended. Hoy was a native of Dunmow and was awarded both flitches which were given by S. Luckin and W. R. Hoskins. Pony racing for the Dunmow Cup, The Flitch of Bacon Cup, The Stewards' Cup, and the Eclipse Stakes. J. T. Neme, of London, provided stage attractions ; Thaxted Brass Band in attendance. Two police sergeants and fifteen constables on duty.

Authority—Essex County Chronicle, 8 August 1890.

3 August 1891

Held in a marquee in a meadow on the Causeway, Great Dunmow.
Judge—J. M. Welch, auctioneer of Great Dunmow.
Jury—Grace Staines, Kate Russell, Lena Brock, Harriet Grout, Blanche Clark, Emily Monkham.
Tom Dalziel, James Randall, Austin Staines, William Staines, Robert Russell, Charles Cook.
Counsel for the claimants—Robert Marsh and Charles Samms.
Counsel for the bacon—F. W. Bartley and G. J. Mackenzie.
Crier of the court—J. Hamilton.
Claimants—Rev. W. C. Wallace, vicar of Shibbear, Highampton, N. Devon, and his wife, both between 35 and 40 years of age.
William Bowen, retired soldier, and later a clerk, of Hounslow, and his wife Ellen Charlotte.
William Robert White, M.D., of Belmont, Wadhurst, Sussex, and his wife.
Attendance—About 600 at the 'trials' including Lord and Lady Algernon Gordon Lennox.
Weather—Sunny, but with a few showers.
Organizers—Local Sports Committee (Chairman—F. J. Snell ; Hon. Sec.— H. Staines).
Notes—Grounds opened at 1 p.m. and jury took their places at 3.15 p.m. Dunmow Brass Band in Hussar uniform under Mr. Martin. Stage performance by a company of London artists.

Authorities—The Star, 4 August 1891 ; *Essex County Chronicle,* 7 August 1891.

1 August 1892

Held in a marquee in a meadow on the Causeway, Great Dunmow.
Judge—J. Cook, of Dunmow.
Jury—Esther Franklin, Lizzie Heard, Nellie Sedgerton [? Ledgerton], Annie
   Portway, Maud Saunders, Alice Smith.
   T. Dalziel, A. Staines, J. Cook, J. Newman, F. J. Nicholls, S. Savill.
Counsel for the claimants—Robert Marsh.
Counsel for the bacon—J. M. Welch.
Crier of the court—J. Hamilton.
Claimants—Joseph Hird, army pensioner, aged 79, and his wife, slightly
   younger, of Turner's Road, Burdett Road, Bow, London.
   Dennis Bridgman, City worker, aged 38, and his wife, aged 33, of
   Tycoe Villa, Allenby Road, Forest Hill, London.
Attendance—Said to be 5,000, including Lord and Lady Brooke, Col.
   Lockwood, M.P., and a distinguished party.
Organizers—Dunmow Flitch Committee.
Notes—Hird and his wife married for 54 years. The Bridgmans
   were married in 1885 at Shibbear, of which parish the vicar
   was a flitch winner in 1891. Flitches presented by G. & R.
   Randall, brewers, of Dunmow, and Fitch & Son, of London.

8 August 1893

Held in a marquee.
Judge—J. M. Welch.
Jury—Emily Gowers, Louisa Gowers, Harriet Grout, Maud Hamilton, Grace
   Hamilton, Grace Staines.
   S. Brain, T. Dalziel, W. Hamilton, C. D. W. King, J. W. Newman,
   Austin Staines.
Counsel for the claimants—Robert Marsh.
Counsel for the bacon—F. W. Bartley.
Crier of the court—James Hamilton.
Claimants—Francis Webb, railway clerk, and his wife, of Needwood Villas,
   Falling Heath, Wednesbury, Staffs.
   Philip Garner, horse slaughterer, aged 30, and his wife, aged 26,
   of West Molesey, Surrey.
Weather—Favourable.
Organizers—Local Committee (Chairman—F. J. Snell; Hon. Sec.—H.
   Staines).
Notes—Mr. Bartley was a director of G. & R. Randall, the Dunmow brewers, but unlike Robert Marsh, had no literary
   pretensions. James Hamilton is described as being dressed in
   resplendent livery. Seven couples applied for the flitch and
   three were selected, but Mr. & Mrs. Parkes of Birmingham
   were prevented from attending owing to the illness of their
   child. They were disappointed at not being present as they
   applied in 1892 at which date they had been married two
   days short of the stipulated period. Braintree Town Band
   played during the day; there were horse and pony races,
   and a firework display in the evening.

Authority—*Essex Standard*, 12 August 1893.

Song of the Flitch.

Come all you gallant Essex men,
  And rally round now pray do,
The flitch is this year claimed again,
  By whom I soon will tell you.
For surely 'tis a glorious plan
  Your wives to love and cherish,
And he that beats them is no man,
  And surely ought to perish.

CHORUS.
  So Essex lads and lasses pray
    'Example now be taking,
  Be off to Church—no longer stay
    And claim the Flitch of Bacon.

One Jerry Heard—a Suffolk man,
  With Sarah for a wife, Sirs,
Have lived together on a plan,
  Without an angry word, Sirs.
For down in Staffordshire they've lived,
  Like Turtle-doves a-cooing,
And ever since they've married been
  Have nothing else been doing.

    Oh, Dunmow is a wondrous place,
      With joy the world is shaken,
    And thousands come from every town,
      To see them claim the bacon.

Policeman Heard, from Staffordshire,
  Have often thieves been taking,
They now may rest a little while
  For he's come to claim the bacon.
And though he's taken many up,
  Perhaps with staff knocked down too,
He's given his wife but staff of life,
  As every man should well do.

    So Essex men where'er you be,
      In every rank or station,
    Oh with your wives lead peaceful lives,
      And you shall all have bacon.

Another claimant, William Sparke,
  Who has his eye on bacon,
From silly Suffolk comes as well,
  And will the Flitch be taking.
He's passed his life in making wheels
  And bodies, too, for coaches,
But never with his loving wife
  Had angry reproaches.

    The other Jeremy O'Brien,
      In his claim there's a flaw,
    For Mrs B., his poor old gal,
      Is just laid in the straw.

That Essex is a wondrous place,
  We all of us are learning,
In Braintree Donkies given away
  To all who cease from swearing.
So swearing men that wop their wives,
  Ought surely to be shaken,
And have water gruel all their lives,
  But not a smell of bacon.

    So with your wives lead peaceful lives
      No angry words be taking,
    And all you single chaps get swished
      And claim the Flitch of Bacon.

If what they say next year is true,
  The hogs may well be quaking,
For half the grunters in the land
  Will soon be Dunmow bacon.
All German soldiers at the Cape,
  That married Essex lasses,
Will come and claim the ancient flitch,
  And ride back on Braintree asses.

    So here's success to Heard and Sparke
      Who've gained their undertaking,
    Their wives shall hug them all their lives
      If fed on Dunmow Bacon.

A BROADSHEET ISSUED IN 1857

FIGURE 8

10 August 1894

Held in a marquee in the Causeway Meadow, Great Dunmow.
Judge—J. M. Welch.
Jury—Maud Hamilton, Grace Hamilton, Hannah Scott, E. J. Clark, Harriet
   Grout, Rose Franklin.
   C. D. W. King, S. Brain, T. Lancaster, W. Monkham, C. Cook,
   R. Franklin.
Counsel for the claimants—Robert Marsh.
Counsel for the bacon—F. W. Bartley.
Crier of the court—James Hamilton.
Claimants—Angelo Fahie, civil and electrical engineer, aged 44, and his
   wife (née Campbell-Lambert of Liston Hall, Essex), of Monkstown,
   Dublin.
   Daniel Welch, railway platelayer, and his wife, of Essendon, Herts.
Organizers—Dunmow Flitch Committee.
Notes—Three couples had been selected from the entrants ; the
   pair who retired from the contest were Mr. & Mrs. Charles
   Binyon, but as members of the Society of Friends, ' the characteristic aversion of their sect to notoriety . . . outweighed
   their ambition '. Entertainments opened with cob and pony
   races, and ended with a firework display. A new operatic
   cantata, "Ye Dunmow Flitch", performed by a choral and
   orchestral company, under the composer, Mr. Daughtry, of
   the *Sheffield Telegraph*, was rendered.
Authorities—*Pall Mall Gazette*, 7 August 1894 ; *Essex County Standard*,
   14 August 1894 ; *The Sketch*, 1 August 1894.

5 August 1895

Held in a marquee in Causeway Meadows, Great Dunmow.
Judge—J. M. Welch.
Jury—Florence Wilder, Agnes Harrison, Grace Ruffel, Emily Warren, Maud
   Goldstone, S. J. Butcher.
   Austin Staines, Stanley Savill, William Monckman, Arthur Stacey,
   George Goodey, George Pocock.
Counsel for the claimants—Robert Marsh.
Counsel for the bacon—T. Gibbons, of Great Dunmow (see *Plate XXI*).
Crier of the court—J. Hamilton.
Claimants—Sergt.-Major Daniel Baker, Yeoman of the Guard, and his wife
   Louisa (née Horner), of Purrett Road, Plumstead, Kent.
   G. Johnson, coach builder, and his wife Jessie Kinnear (née Low),
   of Market Harborough, Leicestershire.
   James Clough, gardener, and his wife (née Newstead), of Surlingham.
Weather—Fine.
Organizers—Committee with R. C. Lyle as Chairman, and H. Staines as
   Hon. Sec.
Notes—Sergt.-Major Baker, born about 1832, wore a resplendent
   ' Polytechnic ' uniform ; his wife, much younger, was in black.
   Baker had seen much overseas service including the Crimea
   and Lucknow. There were pony races, the band of the South
   Metropolitan School, Witham, and a firework display. Over
   £200 was taken for admission to the grounds.
Authority—*Essex County Chronicle*, 9 August 1895.

3 August 1896

Held in a marquee in Causeway Meadows, Great Dunmow.
Judge—Samuel White, of London.
Jury—Annie Bird, Sarah Butcher, Kate Harrison, Edith Harrison, Florence Noon, Annie Reeving.
Sidney Butcher, Frederick Pepper, George Goodey, Harry Preston, Charles Holtz, Percy McGrath.
Counsel for the claimants—Robert Marsh.
Counsel for the bacon—T. Gibbons.
Crier of the court—J. Hamilton.
Claimants—Alfred Drury, servant at Queen's College, Oxford, and his wife, aged 45, of 8 Bliss Court, Broad Street, Oxford.
Henry Johnson, employed by Coppen Bros., Lambeth, and his wife, of 35 Clayton Buildings, Kennington Road, Lambeth, London.
Edward Rooke, retired coachman, and his wife Susanna (née Franklin), of White Cottage, Hailey Lane, Amwell, Herts.
Attendance—5,000, of whom 1,000 witnessed the trials.
Organizers—Dunmow Flitch Committee.
Notes—Mrs. Rooke was a native of Hornchurch, Essex. One flitch was given by Messrs. Randall, Dunmow Brewery, and the other by Messrs. Van den Bergh, of Mincing Lane, London. Mr. G. Lee, sweet-maker, of Thaxted, presented each of the three winning couples with a canister of sweets. Cob and pony racing, stage attractions, the band of the South Metropolitan District School, Witham, and a firework display added to the main event of the day. £261 was taken in admission charges to the fête.
Authority—*Essex County Chronicle*, 7 August 1896.

2 August 1897

Held in a marquee in Causeway Meadows, Great Dunmow.
Judge—Frank Hamilton.
Jury—Edith King, Maud King, Florence Clarke, Mary Mullens, Beatrice Mullens, Mabel Hart.
Austin J. Staines, J. W. Monkman, George Goodey, George Pocock, Walter E. West, Thomas J. Dalziel.
Counsel for the claimants—W. G. Linsell, of Stebbing.
Counsel for the bacon—T. Gibbons.
Clerk of the court—J. Hamilton.
Claimants—Josiah Lambert, gold and silver wire drawer, and later a clerk, aged 74, and his wife Mary (née Norman), aged 70, of Mildmay Road, Islington, London.
George Tayler, carpenter, and his wife Eliza (née Jiggins), of Little Leighs, Essex (see *Plate XXVII*).
Attendance—5,000.
Organizers—Committee with J. Hamilton as Hon. Sec.
Notes—Josiah Lambert, a descendant of John Lambert of Ardleigh, the Cromwellian general (see *Essex County Chronicle*, 23 July 1897), and his wife were married in 1846. Bacon presented by R. & W. Randall, of Dunmow Brewery, and Mr. Woodward of the Great Eastern Railway. The judge and

PLATE XXI

A STAUNCH DEFENDER OF THE BACON !

Mr. (now Colonel) Tom Gibbons who was Counsel for the Bacon, 1895-
1913, and Judge, 1931-8, in a characteristic attitude.

PLATE XXII

THE PRIOR'S CHAIR

This chair (see pp. 59-60) was formerly used for carrying the successful claimants in procession ; the holes through which poles were inserted may be seen below the seat.

A Token issued at Dunmow in 1793, showing a Flitch and a Coat-of-Arms—three Daggers on a blue background.

By the Courtesy of the Trustees of the British Museum.

PLATE XXIII

J. W. ROBERTSON SCOTT, C.H.

Founder, and for many years editor of " The Countryman ", who wrote
The Strange Story of the Dunmow Flitch, and acted the part of Geoffrey
Shether (the last Prior of Dunmow) in the Flitch Pageant, 1912.

PLATE XXIV

THEATRE ROYAL, DRURY-LANE.

FOR THE BENEFIT OF

Mr. PALMER and Mr BELLAMY.

This present WEDNESDAY. June 22, 1814,
Their Majesties Servants will perform SHAKSPEARE's Comedy of

Twelfth Night.

Orsino, Mr. H O L L A N D,
Sebastian. Mr. I. WALLACK, Antonio, Mr. R. PHILLIPS,
Valentine, Mr. CROOKE, Curio, Mr. COOKE.
Sir Toby Belch, Mr. P A L M E R.
Sir Andrew Ague Cheek, Mr. L O V E G R O V E,
Sea Captain, Mr. WALDEGRAVE, Fabian, Mr. FISHER,
Ma'volio, Mr. D O W T O N.
Priest Mr. MADDOCKS, Officers, Mr. I. WEST, Mr. EVANS.
Olivia, Mrs. G L O V E R, Maria Miss M E L L O N,
Viola, Miss S T A N L E Y.
(Being her Second Appearance in that Character.)
At the End of the Play,

A RUSSIAN PAS DEUX,

By Mr. OSCAR BYRNE and Miss SMITH.

In the Course of the Evening,
The PICTURE of a PLAY-HOUSE; or, BUCKS HAVE AT YE ALL,
will be spoken *(for the first time in this Theatre)* by Mr. PALMER.

Mr. PYNE will sing a popular New Song called *"England & our brave Allies."*

Mr BELLAMY will sing *"Our Laws, Wives and Liberty."*
And by particular desire, the celebrated Song of *"The WOLF."*

And by desire the YORKSHIRE RECITATION of
Richard and Betty at Hickleton Fair, by Mr. KNIGHT.

To which will be added (Never acted at this Theatre) a Musical Entertainment called the

Flitch of Bacon.

Major Benbow, Mr. DOWTON, Justice Benbow, Mr. R. PHILLIPS,
Captain Greville, Mr. P H I L I P P S,
In which Character he will introduce the admired Song of
"EVELYN's BOWER," (from the IRISH MELODIES.)
Captain Wilson, Mr. B E L L A M Y, Tipple, Mr. M U N D E N.
Eliza, Mrs. M O U N T A I N,
In which character she will introduce the favorite Scotch song
"JENNY TO THE GREEN."
VIVANT REX ET REGINA.   NO MONEY TO BE RETURNED.   [C.Lowndes, Printer, Marquis Court, London.

The Publick are respectfully informed, that the Tragedy of KING RICHARD the
THIRD will be repeated once a Week. Due Notice will be given of Mr. KEAN's
next Performances in the MERCHANT of VENICE, and HAMLET.

Mr. KEAN's Performances of OTHELLO and IAGO will be repeated alternately, every *Thursday*
and *Saturday.* On the Thursdays, *Othello,* on the Saturdays, *Iago.*
The numerous Parties who have enquired concerning the next Representation of the Splendid
Oriental Romance of ILLUSION; or, the TRANCES OF NOURJAHAD, are respect-
fully informed that it will be repeated, for the 40th time
To-morrow, after SHAKSPEARE's Tragedy of OTHELLO, *Othello,* Mr. KEAN.
On *Friday,* the Comedy of RICHES, or *The Wife and Brother Luke,* (4th time) Mr. KEAN.
Being the last time of his performing that Character this Season. With (3d time) the last New
Dance of AULD ROBIN GRAY, and (3d time) the New Farce of FAIR CHEATING.
On *Saturday,* OTHELLO. *Othello,* Mr. RAE, *Iago,* Mr. KEAN. To which will be added,
a favourite Musical Farce.
On *Monday,* (22 l time) SHAKSPEARE's Tragedy of KING RICHARD the THIRD.
King Richard, Mr. KEAN.
With (4th time) AULD ROBIN GRAY, and (15th time) INTRIGUE.
The Performances of the New and highly popular Melo-Dramatick Romance of
the WOODMAN's HUT are unavoidably suspended, owing to the severe Indisposition of
Miss KELLY, until further Notice.

Playbill advertising a performance of 'The Flitch of Bacon' at
the Theatre Royal, Drury Lane, 1814.

counsel rode in the procession in a motor car lent by the London Motor Van and Wagon Company, while the jury and other officers were conveyed in brakes and wagonettes. There were cob and pony races, a clown cricket match, clown donkey races, roundabouts, and a firework display. Witham School Band in attendance. Mr. Robert Marsh who had acted as counsel for the claimants on several occasions died before this 'trial'; he was famed for his apt Shakespearian quotations. Over six hundred people arrived in Dunmow by train on the Saturday preceding the festivities, and over nine hundred on the Monday. The receipts amounted to £230.

Authorities—Essex County Chronicle, 6 August 1897; *Daily Mail,* 2 and 3 August 1897.

1 August 1898

Held in marquee in Causeway Meadows, Great Dunmow.
Judge—F. W. Bartley.
Jury—Florence Wright, Eleanor Roydhouse, Lily Rose, Nellie Matthams, Ethel Pritchard, Ellen Adams.
    Sidney Linsell, Frederick Colina, Harry Hales, Harry Barber, William Smith, Edgar Luckin.
Counsel for the claimants—W. G. Linsell.
Counsel for the bacon—T. Gibbons.
Crier of the court—J. Hamilton.
Claimants—Frederick Herbert, dealer in antique furniture, and his wife, Elizabeth, of Hounslow, Middlesex.
    James Frost, church clerk and verger, and his wife, of Sutton, Surrey.
Weather—Fine and hot.
Attendance—Large.   Up to 2.30 p.m., 1,087 passengers had alighted at Dunmow railway station.
Organizers—Committee with James Hamilton as secretary.
Notes—One of the flitches presented by R. & W. Randall. Band of Witham S.M.D. School in attendance. Main attractions were horse-racing and firework display.
Authority—Essex County Chronicle, 5 August 1898.

7 August 1899

Held in a marquee.
Judge—J. V. Mackenzie.
Jury—Florence Wright, Annie Bailey, Lily Rose, Nellie Matthams, Maud Smith, Edith Gibbs.
    S. Linsell, H. Matthams, Frederick Plomer, Charles Day, Thomas Gammage, Edgar Luckin.
Counsel for the claimants—W. G. Linsell.
Counsel for the bacon—T. Gibbons.
Clerk of the court, and Marshal—J. Hamilton.
Claimants—Sergt. Alexander McCulloch, aged 66, and his wife, aged 38, of Norwich.
    Frederick Bennett, painter, aged 29, and his wife, aged 27, of Heathfield House, Wandsworth Common, Surrey.
Organizers—Committee with Frederick J. Snell as Chairman, and J. Hamilton as Secretary.

G

Notes—There was a preliminary examination by the organizing committee. Bacon given by J. J. and H. E. Pryor, of Palmer's Stores, Hammersmith, who were natives of Dunmow. Military tournament and cavalry display by 7th Yeomanry Brigade ; band of the S.M.D. School, Witham ; stage attractions and concert in the evening. McCulloch's father was guard on the old convict ship ' Emperor Alexander ', and the claimant was born during a voyage to Botany Bay with a load of convicts ; he held the medal of the Royal Humane Society. Bennett and his wife did *not* win the bacon as the jury were of the opinion ' that there was an absence of love when there was an empty stomach ' ; the press account infers, however, that they were given the bacon although not as an award of the Court.

Authority—Essex County Chronicle, 11 August 1899.

6 August 1900

Held in marquee.

Judge—James V. Mackenzie.

Jury—Florence Burgoyne, Edith Gibbs, Nellie Hipkiss, Mary Townrow, Cissie Turner, Minnie Reid.

Thomas Brazier, William Clark, Harold Plomer, Arthur Stacey, Jack Turner, Arthur Wilton.

Counsel for the claimants—W. G. Linsell.

Counsel for the bacon—T. Gibbons.

Clerk of the court—J. Hamilton.

Claimants—Evelyn John Evatt, medical student, and his wife (née Scott), of Newcastle.

James Munnings, gardener, and his wife Sarah Ann, of Pinner.

Weather—Wet.

Attendance—Good crowd in marquee, but very few for outdoor attractions.

Organizers—Dunmow Flitch Committee.

Notes—Flitches given by the William Davis Co., London. Horse racing was main outdoor event.

Authority—Essex County Standard, 10 August 1900.

5 August 1901

Held in Causeway Meadows, Great Dunmow.

Judge—F. Lewis, ironmonger, of Great Dunmow.

Jury—Florence Burton, Ethel Turpin, Alice Smith, Gertrude Colyer, Alice Binnie, Margarita Clarke.

John Brazier, Samuel Love, Thomas Brazier, Richard Roper, William Brazier, Robert W. Clarke.

Counsel for the claimants—James V. Mackenzie

Counsel for the bacon—T. Gibbons.

Clerk of the court—James Hamilton.

Claimants—James Owers Devereux, chemist's assistant, aged 37, and his wife Kate, of 62, Nelson Square, Southwark, London.

Herbert Edgar Clarke (a native of Dunmow), journeyman baker, and his wife Amelia Elizabeth, of Stepney, London.

Weather—Favourable.

Attendance—Nearly 8,000.

Notes—The speeches of counsel in these 'trials' were particularly
eloquent ; the claimants produced testimonials from their
friends as to their happy married state. Flitches presented
by Bovril Ltd., together with a case of the special product of
that firm for each competitor. Other attractions included pony
racing, and music by the Dunmow Town Band. Receipts for
the day amounted to £300.

Authority—*Essex County Chronicle,* 9 August 1901.

4 August 1902

Held in marquee.
Judge—James V. Mackenzie.
Jury—Misses M. L. Miller, Walsham, Taylor, A. Binnie, L. Bennett, B.
Markwell.
Messrs. E. J. Bird, E. Wright, L. Wright, W. Brazier, Robinson,
S. Lee.
Counsel for the claimants—W. G. Linsell.
Counsel for the bacon—T. Gibbons.
Crier of the court—C. W. D. King.
Claimants—George H. Wallis, wine merchant, and his wife Mary Edith
(née Mann), of Derby.
Alfred Brook, waterworks inspector, and his wife Alice (née Pennall),
of Bromley, Kent.
Weather—Showery.
Attendance—Said to be a record ; the marquee held 1,500 people.
Organizers—Dunmow Flitch Committee.

Notes—Mrs. Wallis was a native of Colchester. After the ceremony,
there was pony racing, a fair, gymnastic and acrobatic performances, and fireworks in the evening. Band of the Essex
Regiment in attendance.

Authority—*Essex County Chronicle,* 8 August 1902.

3 August 1903

Held in marquee in Causeway Meadows, Great Dunmow.
Judge—F. W. Bartley, of Brighton, formerly of Dunmow.
Jury—Ethel Green, Florence Green, Dora Eveline Vessey, Chrissie
Turner, Lydia Housden, Nellie L. Gould.
Frank Hugh Clark, Harry Clark, Sidney Markwell, Jack Turner,
Bert Franklin, John Snow.
Counsel for the claimants—W. G. Linsell.
Counsel for the bacon—T. Gibbons.
Crier of the court—C. W. D. King.
Claimants—J. C. Keeble, carver and gilder, and his wife, of Northampton.
W. L. Jackaman, clerk, and his wife (née Middleton), of Felixstowe.
Attendance—Large ; the marquee held over 1,000 people.
Organizers—Dunmow Flitch Committee.

Notes—Mr. & Mrs. Jackaman were married in 1870, and the lady
was a native of Twinstead, Essex. There were three dozen
claimants. When the judge took his seat, the bottom of his

chair fell through, and his legs shot into the air ! Programme of horse-racing, gymnastics and nigger minstrels ; Band of the 2nd Norfolks in attendance. Dunmow grocers report large sales of ham and bacon to visitors. Twenty-two police on duty, and excellent order maintained in the gaily decorated streets, and on the ground.

Authority—*Essex County Chronicle, 7 August 1903.*

1 August 1904

Held in marquee in meadows near the Causeway, Great Dunmow.
Judge—F. W. Bartley.
Jury—Hetty Errington, Mary Sheen, Kate Saunders, Flora Harris, Edith Chivers, Florence Saunders.
William Sparks, Harold Kemp, Frederick Haynes, Sidney Thorogood, Frederick Coombe Harris, Albert Rowley.
Counsel for the claimants—Samuel Humphreys, of Cricklewood.
Counsel for the bacon—T. Gibbons.
Crier of the court—C. W. D. King.
Claimants—Christopher Holford, independent, and his wife (née Skilliter), of Putney, London.
James Quiggin, shoemaker, and his wife Margaret (née Coughlan), of Marylebone, London.
Attendance—Large ; the marquee held 2,000 people.
Organizers—Dunmow Flitch Committee.
Notes—Forty couples applied for the Flitch. Mr. and Mrs. Quiggin were married at a Registry Office, but the judge allowed them to take the oath without alteration. Horse and pony racing. Bishop's Stortford Town Band in attendance.
Authority—*Essex County Chronicle, 5 August 1904.*

19 July 1905

Held in marquee in Causeway Meadows.
Judge—A. E. Floyd, of Bishop's Stortford.
Jury—Kate Daffarn, Nellie Gould, Mabel Philo, Hilda Rhind, Ellen Walshaw, Dolly Rhodes.
Ashton Bensley, William Daffarn, George Gunthorpe, Arthur Joslin, P. Prideaux, Ernest Wright.
Counsel for the claimants—J. V. Mackenzie.
Counsel for the bacon—T. Gibbons.
Crier of the court—C. W. D. King.
Claimants—Owen Francis Samuel Partridge Jenkins, retired clergyman, and his wife Elizabeth, of St. John's, Mold, Flintshire.
Frederick John Garbett Noakes, quarry engineer, and his wife, Eva Jane, of 17 Bedlam, Bitterley, Ludlow, Salop.
Attendance—Many thousands.
Organizers—Dunmow Flitch Committee.
Notes—Nearly one hundred applications were received. Rev. and Mrs. Jenkins were married in 1869. Judge, jury and counsel were all unmarried. Attractions included horse racing and jumping, and baby show. Band of the King's Own Scottish Borderers in attendance. Police reported a ' plague ' of pick-

pockets. A Flitch ceremony held in New York this year ; on the souvenir are these words :

Whereas :

Walter Girdwood Mulliner and Gabrielle his wife, in reverence for the old tradition, its quaint basic thought so sweetly resting in the sanctity of the marriage relation, knowing in their hearts that they have earned the " Flitch of Bacon " by the sure right of their living, although far from the Priory and the pointed stones, do here and now kneel and lay claim to it.

I, Leslie Allen Wright, the chief attendant to the Bridegroom upon his day of wedding, praying a grace of pardon for usurping the Prior's rightful duty, yet feeling the fine prompting spirit of the ancient custom, do now bestow upon these two worthy persons, Walter Girdwood Mulliner and Gabrielle his wife, a Flitch of Bacon.

May they in all the added years of their life, grow in Ripeness and in Spirit. Amen.

New York, September 26th, 1905.

Authorities—Essex County Chronicle, 21 July 1905 ; *The Mentor* (New York), October, 1928.

6 August 1906

Held in marquee in a meadow at the back of Dunmow Workhouse.

Judge—J. Keith Sheppard, of Chelmsford.

Jury—Ada Tuttleby, Ethel Collett, Mabel Barnard, Nellie Sanders, Dora Bradley, Edith Lucking.

William Import, Frederick Levitt, Frederick Staines, George Meacock, Richard Snow, James Johnston.

Counsel for the claimants—James V. Mackenzie.

Counsel for the bacon—T. Gibbons.

Claimants—Walter Stephen James Lloyd-Willey, manager of T. Hill Jones (charcoal merchants), and his wife Gertrude Augusta (dau. of Hon. John Storey), of 5 Cottage Grove, Bow, London.

Henry Lewis Morgan, I.S.O., retired from Ordnance Survey Office, and his wife Katherine Mary, of 517 Cliff Road, Bristol.

Attendance—No figures, but said to be good.

Organizers—The Flitch Committee (Chairman—John Wright ; Douglas Bayly of White Lion Inn, Great Dunmow, Hon. Sec.).

Notes—Seats in the marquee 2/6 and 1/-. Very long speeches in this trial. Amusements included horse jumping, donkey races, beauty show (1st prize, 30/-, won by Ethel Collett of Three Ashes Inn, Takeley ; 2nd prize, 20/-, by Miss Gray of Great Easton ; 3rd prize, 10/-, by Miss Saunders of Little Easton), baby show, stage attraction by London artistes, and open air display of animated photographs in the evening. Dunmow Excelsior Band, conducted by A. G. Cornell, in attendance. Prebendary Carlile, founder of the Church Army, preached on the Dunmow Flitch, at St. Mary-at-Hill, Billingsgate, London, on 5 Aug. 1906, and said that the trial ' quaint and humourous as it was in many of its aspects, served to emphasise many wholesome lessons '.

Authority—Essex County Chronicle, 10 August 1906.

DUNMOW FLITCH OF BACON !

Come all you lads and lasses fair
  And cheer this undertaking,
And with your wives lead peaceful lives,
  And get the Flitch of Bacon.
This Dunmow is a precious place,
  Renowed through England wide O ;
And France as well, who, strange to tell,
  Now claims the Flitch with pride O.

Then cheer up boys for Dunmow's joys,
  Your hearts no longer aching,
And never wop your wives again,
  And feed them well on Bacon.

No more have jars or angry wars
  With your kind precious spouses,
And let them do just as they please,
  Yes, even wear your trousers ;
And all you single chaps and girls
  Your marriage vows be taking,
Get all your rhubarbs planted in,
  And claim the Flitch of Bacon.

Give all your money to your wives,
  Don't ask them how they've spent it,
For if you do, depend upon't,
  You surely will repent it ;
For in the Union no man now
  His wife need now be taking,
But lead a jolly peaceful life,
  And live on Dunmow Bacon.

A Frencham has been bold enough
  To try this undertaking,
And all the way from France has come
  To claim the Flitch of Bacon.
One twelvemonth long no angry words
  Or quarrels have they taken,
And now the Frenchman and his wife
  Shall have some British Bacon.

The very hogs for miles around
  Now in their styes are quaking
And squeaking to each other cry,
  O damn the Flitch of Bacon ;
For every poor man in the land
  No pigs' stye need be making,
But lead with wife a peaceful life
  And claim the Flitch of Bacon,

So all you Essex wives and maids,
  Your sides with laughter shaking,
You all shall have a bussel made
  Out of a Flitch of Bacon.
And all you sorry single chaps
  In batchelors' situation,
Come to the altar, lead the dears,
  And give 'em Dunmow Bacon.

Your children like the olive tree
  Shall grow, and soon be taking
To plough and drive, and laughing thrive
  On beer, and bread, and Bacon.
And if your wives bad tempered are,
  And airs on them be taking,
You soon will bring them peaceful round
  If you just stop their Bacon,

And in conclusion, married men,
  In every grade and station,
Get all the children that you c an
  To beat the Russian nation.
And three cheers for the blessed man
  Who raised this undertaking,
His name it shall for ever live
  And be engraved on Bacon.

————

Another example of a Broadsheet sold at a Flitch Trial. Note the reference
to the Bacon having been won by Le Chevalier and Madame de Chatelain
in 1855.

FIGURE 9

5 August 1912

Held in a marquee in Parsonage Meadows, Great Dunmow.
Judge—A. E. Floyd, solicitor, of Great Dunmow.
Jury—Misses G. Bateman, I. Errington, L. Power, G. Pannell, M. Willett, I. Wright.
Messrs. Stacey B. King, C. Andrews, W. R. Lewis, S. Pannell, F. Power, F. Willett.
Counsel for the claimants—James V. Mackenzie.
Counsel for the bacon—T. Gibbons.
Clerk of the court—W. H. Mills.
Crier of the court—George Saunders.
Claimants—Harry Smith, successively schoolmaster, barber, sub-postmaster and grocer, and his wife Annie, of Crewton, Derby.
Lewis Frank Butcher, butcher, and then traveller, born at Tilty, and his wife Harriett Newberry, of 45 St. James' Road, Brixton, London.
Weather—Favourable.
Attendance—Very large. Three hundred people in the procession.
Organizers—Committee with the Earl of Warwick as president, A. E. Floyd as chairman of Executive Committee, Carl Anderson as secretary.
Notes—Thirty couples applied, but only two accepted. Pageant arranged by Hugh Cranmer-Byng, included representations of numerous persons closely connected with Great and Little Dunmow; the part of Geoffrey Shether (the last prior) was taken by J. W. Robertson Scott (see *Plate XXIII*). Band of the Essex Yeomanry in attendance. Day ended with Morris dancing and firework display. Bacon presented by the Dunmow Flitch Bacon Company which had opened its factory in Dunmow in October 1909. Long correspondence in county newspapers between Rev. J. F. Stephenson and J. W. Robertson Scott about the ceremony not being held at Little Dunmow. A trial was held at Ilford this year.
Authorities—*Daily Express*, 6 August 1912; *Daily Sketch*, 6 August 1912 (with good pictures of the winners, court officers, and pony races); *Essex County Standard*, 10 August 1912; *Essex County Chronicle*, 9 August 1912.

4 August 1913

Held in a marquee near the Downs, Great Dunmow.
Judge—M. H. Ryan, of Ilford.
Jury—Misses L. Simmons, Errington, D. Stokes, Slater, C. J. Day, F. Gallon.
Messrs. A. Byford, A. Ayton, C. Coates, C. Wright, G. Sproul, L. H. Floyd.
Counsel for the claimants—James V. Mackenzie.
Counsel for the bacon—T. Gibbons.
Clerk of the court—Carl Anderson.
Crier of the court—George Saunders.
Claimants—William Hewett, clerk, and his wife Agnes, of 12 Howard Street, York.
Littlejohn Wood, fitter, aged 30, and his wife Lily Rose, of 14 Elthorne Road, Upper Holloway, London.
Organizers—Committee with W. R. Errington as Hon. Sec.
Notes—Singing competition in the evening and dancing to the Arc

Work Prize Silver Band, of Chelmsford, in place of pageant procession held in previous year. Mr. Mackenzie described as having a bombastic style and employing a good deal of rhetoric ; Mr. Gibbons, cross and foreboding (!), yet with a waggishness that Dunmow highly appreciated (see *Plate XXI*). Bacon given by the Dunmow Flitch Bacon Company. Horse racing and other sports.

Authority—Essex County Chronicle, 3 and 8 August 1913.

4 August 1930

Held in a marquee in the Causeway Meadow, Great Dunmow.

Judge—Geoffrey Tyndale.

Jury—Misses M. Savill, C. Folger, I. Clark, P. Ward, D. Sewell, H. Hampton.
Messrs. E. Hunt, L. Richardson, Metcalf, Foster, M. Butcher, C. Spurgeon.

Counsel for the claimants—Edward S. T. Davies.

Counsel for the bacon—Arthur Mortimer.

Clerk of the court—George Saunders.

Crier of the court—R. Michelson.

Claimants—William Edwards, solicitor's managing clerk, and his wife Amy Eliza, of New Street, Great Dunmow.
Frederick William Goodey, postman, and his wife Winifred D., of Cox Hill, Great Easton, Essex.
E. W. Walker, accountant, and his wife Ivy, of Rushdene, The Downs, Great Dunmow.
—Vincent, piano tuner, and his wife Agnes, of 9 Weight Road, Chelmsford.

Weather—Adverse.   *Attendance*—5,000.

Notes—First trials since 1913. Two separate ceremonies. Flitches (given by Alderman A. M. Mathews, J.P.) awarded to Goodey and Walker while gammons were given to the other competitors. Receipts—£270 ; profit to the Liberal Association and the League of Nations' Union funds. Community singing, dance, confetti battle, and firework display. Goodey delivered a rasher of bacon to every house on his round the next morning. ' Trials ' held at Ilford in 1920, 1929, 1930 and 1932, and at the Palace Theatre, London, in 1924. The Ilford Trial of Whit-Monday 1930, was the subject of a cartoon by Tom Webster in the *Daily Mail*. The Ilford ' trials ' aroused a good deal of comment in Dunmow ; one inhabitant is reported to have said ' You might as well take Barnet Fair to Southampton, or row the 'Varsity boat-race on the Clyde, as take the Flitch Trial to Ilford '. A bacon-factory worker gave his opinion in these words : ' Oi down't reckon oi know where this ole Ilford plice is ; oi count that must be somewhere out furrin. Ilford ? Never he'erd tell on't '. Among other places where ' trials ' have been held, Tunbridge Wells

' A Representation of the Antient Custom of Delivering the Gammon of Bacon at the Priory of Dunmow-Parva in Essex.' From a rare broadsheet, published in 1751, giving a short history of the custom and details of the winners of the bacon.

PLATE XXVI

A painting by an unknown artist, in the possession of the Dunmow Rural District Council. The scene is an imaginary one

and Oulton Broad may be mentioned. At Gravesend, a humourous 'trial' was held with an award being made to the unhappiest couple ; male claimants were swathed in bandages, and their wives appeared with black eyes ! At Stainland, in Yorkshire, is, or was, a "Henpecked Club" which holds an annual dumpling dinner ; membership is limited to those who can give positive assurance that they are henpecked. On 5 August 1925, a Pageant of the Dunmow Flitch, with 80 performers, was held at Felsted under the direction of Lt. Col. G. J. Hornsby Wright.

Authorities—*Essex Chronicle*, 24 May 1929, 8 August 1930 ; *St. Martins-le-Grand* [Post Office Magazine], October 1931 ; *Daily Express*, 25 May 1920, 4 April 1924.

3 August 1931

Held in marquee in Causeway Meadows, Great Dunmow.
Judge—Col. T. Gibbons, D.S.O., D.L., J.P.
Jury—Misses J. McRay, M. E. Hampton, D. Sewell, M. Bailey, Callingham, M. Butcher.
Messrs. C. S. L. Sutthery, L. J. Rammage, J. Baines, J. Farrington, F. G. Clarke, H. B. Gardner.
Counsel for the claimants—G. F. Emery.
Counsel for the bacon—Arthur Mortimer and Miss Alsa W. Rhodes.
Chaplain—Rev. P. E. T. Widdrington, M.A.
Clerk of the court—E. S. T. Davies.
Crier of the court—John Gibbons.
Claimants—Alfred Henry Cox, hair-dresser, and his wife Dorothy Elsie, of 62 Chepstow Villas, London.
G. E. Hodgetts, motor mechanic, and his wife, of 31a Bronsart Road, Fulham, London.
Edward Herbert Devoil, platelayer, and his wife Winifred Jessie, of Railway Cottages, Great Dunmow.
Weather—Fine.   *Attendance*—Estimated at over 6,000.
Organizers—Committee with F. Attwater Lewis as Chairman, and F. H. Gale as Hon Sec.
Notes—The trial of Mr. and Mrs. Cox was broadcast, and a sound film made. Flitches presented to the couples by the Chairman of the organizing committee. Attractions included display of horsemanship by Metropolitan Police officers ; ankle competition ; fancy dress parade ; balloon race competition in which over 1,300 balloons were dispatched ; dancing ; firework display. Sawbridgeworth Band in attendance.
Authority—*Essex Chronicle*, 7 August 1931.

1 August 1932

Held in marquee in Causeway Meadows, Great Dunmow.
Judge—Col. T. Gibbons, D.S.O., D.L., J.P.
Jury—Joan MacRae, Ina MacRae, Marjorie Callingham, Madeline Robinson, Muriel French, Mercia Bayly.

H

Cecil Sutthery, Robert Fry, John Baines, Norris Davey, Percy Baldrey, Patrick Widdrington.

Counsel for the claimants—Edward S. T. Davies.

Counsel for the bacon—Philip Guedalla, J.P.

Chaplain—Rev. P. E. T. Widdrington, M.A.

Clerk of the court—H. J. Smith.

Crier of the court—John Gibbons.

Claimants—Andrew Sams, milkman, and his wife, of Station Road, Great Dunmow.

Frederick William Potter, collector for an electricity company, and his wife, Lucy Louisa of Aberfeldy Street, Poplar, London, E.

Samuel Gilbert Nicholls, fancy bazaar proprietor, and his wife, Elizabeth Rose (née Bragg), of Axminster, Devon.

Weather—Severe thunderstorm in the afternoon.

Attendance—4,000.

Organizers—Committee with F. H. Gale as Hon. Sec., F. Culf as Assistant Sec., and Stanley Spore as stage manager.

Notes—The 'trial' of Mr. and Mrs. Potter was broadcast. Mr. Philip Guedalla was the celebrated writer who lived at H. G. Wells' old home, The Laundry, Easton Park, Great Dunmow; he objected to Mr. Mathison, one of the jury, because he was a relative of Mr. and Mrs. Sams. Bishop's Stortford Band in attendance. Boxing displays, fancy dress parade, balloon racing, concert, and firework display among the attractions. 'Trials' also held at Brightlingsea and South Benfleet on the same day.

Authorities—*Daily Sketch*, 2 August 1932 ; *Essex Chronicle*, 5 August 1932.

7 August 1933

Held in a marquee, 160 feet x 40 feet, in Causeway Meadows, Great Dunmow.

Judge—Col. T. Gibbons, D.S.O., D.L., J.P.

Jury—Mercia Bayly, Mona Lawrence, Kitty Pulford, Madeline Robinson, Kathleen Stacey, Peggy Wilkinson.

Cecil Sutthery, John Baines, Percy Baldry, Cecil Clarke, Leslie Eves, Douglas Nicholls.

Counsel for the claimants—A. E. Floyd and E. A. Williams.

Counsel for the bacon—Arthur Mortimer, of Grays Inn, and F. J. H. Snyders.

Chaplain—Rev. P. E. T. Widdrington, M.A.

Clerk of the court—H. J. Smith.

Crier of the court—John Gibbons.

Claimants—E. C. Cox, aged 50, omnibus inspector, and his wife, aged 50, of 13 Keston Road, Peckham, London.

Edwin Mann, aged 51, butler, and his wife, aged 44, cook, of Woking, Surrey.

G. E. Bird, aged 73, commercial traveller, and his wife, of Carthen House, 26 Aldersley Road, Hammersmith, London.

Weather—Very hot.

Attendance—About 2,000.

Organizers—Committee, with Frank Cock, president ; F. C. Culf, hon. sec. ; A. T. Stoddart, hon. treas.

Notes—Numerous claimants. The 'trial' of Mr. and Mrs. Bird broadcast by B.B.C. and National Broadcasting Co. of America. Judge deprecated ' trials ' held at Ilford and elsewhere which were advertised as the original Dunmow Flitch Trials. Rev. P. E. T. Widdrington gave a short history of the ceremony and said it was first instituted to correct a moral evil, and later reinstituted to uphold the ideal of marriage. Band of the 2nd Battalion the Black Watch in attendance. Other attractions included a pony gymkhana, boxing exhibition, balloon race, carnival, fun fair and firework display. Dunmow streets gaily decorated. ' Trials ' also held at Hertford.

Authority—Essex Weekly News, 11 August 1933.

22 April 1935

Held at Foakes Memorial Hall, Great Dunmow.
Judge—Col. T. Gibbons, D.S.O., D.L., J.P.
Jury—Gladys Heppell, Mona Lawrence, Ruth Staines, Kathleen Stacey, Evelyn Ward, Peggy Wilkinson.
    Morton Bailey, John Baines, Leslie Eves, Douglas Nichols, Ernest Percy, John Reeve.
Counsel for the claimants—F. N. Wingent, of Chelmsford.
Counsel for the bacon—E. S. T. Davies.
Chaplain—Rev. P. E. T. Widdrington, M.A.
Clerk of the court—H. S. Spore.
Crier of the court—N. G. Davey.
Claimants—Ernest John Wells, and his wife Lucy Elizabeth, of New Cross Gate, London.
    Mr. and Mrs. R. Evans, of Lower Clapton, London.
    Mr. and Mrs. G. W. McKaig, of Brunswick Square, London.
Attendance—Large.
Notes—The ' trial ' of Mr. and Mrs. Evans was broadcast. The Wells had been married 48 years. Gross takings, including the dance, £65 ; Sawbridgeworth Silver Band in attendance.
Authorities—Essex Review, vol. xliv ; *Essex Chronicle,* 26 April 1935.

6 June 1938

Held at Foakes Memorial Hall, Great Dunmow.
Judge—Col. T. Gibbons, D.S.O., D.L., J.P.
Jury—Daphne Ayres, Elsie Bailey, Beryl Brooks, Elsie Klee, Olive Lipson, Evelyne Thompson.
    Morton Bailey, Ian Hume, Kenneth Lipson, David Luckin, John Nicholls, Geoffrey Taylor.
Counsel for the claimants—F. J. Collinge.
Counsel for the bacon—Edward S. T. Davies.
Chaplain—Rev. W. G. L. Armstrong.
Clerk of the court—H. J. Smith.
Crier of the court—N. G. Davey.
Claimants—Mr. and Mrs. J. Bancroft, of Newton Green, Great Dunmow.
    Mr. and Mrs. R. Compton, of Woodcote, Stradishall, Suffolk.
    Mr. and Mrs. H. V. Clark, of The White Horse, Great Dunmow.
    Mr. and Mrs. C. W. Garner, of The Hanbury Arms, Islington.

Notes—Flitches presented by W. Culpin after the procession at 8.30 p.m.

Authority—*East Anglian Magazine*, September 1949.

1 October 1949

Held in Foakes Memorial Hall, Great Dunmow.

Judge—Kingsley Martin, editor of *New Statesman and Nation*.

Jury—Jeanette Bennett, Jill Coates, Rita Fenn, June Finch, Barbara Purkiss, Sheila Saunders.

William J. Harris, John Armstrong, Vernon Baldry, Antony Hayward, Kenneth Luckin, Douglas May.

Counsel for the claimants—H. J. Smith.

Counsel for the bacon—E. R. St. Aubrey Davies.

Junior Counsel—N. G. Davey.

Chaplain—Canon P. E. T. Widdrington, D.D.

Clerk of the court—J. Gordon Shergold, LL.B.

Crier of the court—William D. Dixon.

Claimants—Mr. and Mrs. T. C. Cocker, of 135 Highfield Lane, Newbold, Chesterfield.

Mr. and Mrs. G. E. Hunt, of Claremont, St. John's Road, Tyler's Green, Penn, Bucks.

W. J. Laws, innkeeper, and his wife, of The Star Inn, Great Dunmow.

L. E. Shelley, and his wife Gladys, of Gladrena, Windmill Lane, Wightwick, Wolverhampton.

Weather—Favourable.

Attendance—Very large.

Organizers—Dunmow Flitch Committee (Hon. Sec.—F. C. Culf, of Great Dunmow).

Notes—There were 60 applicants who had to complete a formidable questionnaire. Gammons of bacon presented by New Zealand through the Commonwealth Gift Scheme. Parts of the ceremonies were televised. Witham British Legion Band, and trumpeters of the King Edward VI Grammar School Cadets (Chelmsford) in attendance. Dance held in the evening. Mr. and Mrs. Hunt married for 43 years. Couples ' chaired ' in replicas of the Prior's chair by ' waggoners ' in traditional Essex smocks. ' Trials ' also held at Great Leighs, 1945, at Ilfracombe, and Palmer's Green, London, in 1949. At Willesborough, Kent, a trial similar to the Dunmow Flitch was held in January, 1950, when the prize was a goose. In *The Times* of 5 September 1941 a correspondent referred to Dunmow in connection with the matrimonial customs of Castelo Melhor in Portugal ; although the analogy is a little far-fetched, it illustrates that the Dunmow custom is a household word. [Thanks to L. M. Wulcko].

Authorities—*The Times*, 19 August 1949 and 3 October 1949 ; *The Star*, 8 September 1949 ; *Evening Standard*, 20 and 22 August 1949 ; *Essex Chronicle*, 25 May 1945, 7 October 1949 ; *Essex Weekly News*, 7 October 1949 ; *The Smoker*, November 1949.

CHAPTER IX

THE KNEELING STONES AND THE PRIOR'S CHAIR

The climax of the Flitch ceremony has always been the taking of the oath (see p. 15) by the persons who have proved their claim to the bacon. Tradition affirms that two great stones lying near the door of Little Dunmow church were used for this purpose, but if they were the two sharply-pointed stones shown on the prints of the Shakeshafts taking the oath (*Plate XXV*), they have long since disappeared ; modern couples kneel on blocks fashioned with a view to comfort. No doubt special stones were kept in or near the priory church in the old days, and it is a fact that there is an ancient stone there to this day which is believed by the credulous to be the one on which claimants formerly knelt. This story must be discredited, because the 'stones', fashioned out of one piece of masonry, are nothing more or less than the bases of a pair of slender columns salvaged from the priory buildings ; they certainly cannot be termed either great or sharp, and are hardly likely to be those about which Dugdale says (see p. 3) that, owing to the length of the ceremony, it must be painful to the claimant to kneel so long on them.

After the 'trials', the fortunate pilgrim—replaced in later days by the winning couples—was carried in procession in the prior's chair described by F. Roe in *Ancient Church Chests and Chairs* (1929), as a venerable thirteenth-century stall which has had the back cut down in height, and the sweeping lines of the arms abbreviated at some later period. 'Such carvings as it possesses', says Mr. Roe, 'are singularly pure in design. The shafts which support the elbow-rests are attachments, as is also the trefoil heading on its back . . . . . This time-worn object is well looked after nowadays, and there is no chance whatever of its being used for any more travesties of the "custom"'. There is every reason to believe that the back of the stall is made up of fifteenth-century work.

It would appear that unless Sherwin's engraving (see *Plate VII*) is incorrect, the stall, now to be seen near the altar in Little Dunmow church, has not been put to an ignominious use since before 1701 ; evidence of its use before that date is provided by the holes beneath the seat where poles were passed through to enable the chair and its occupant(s) to be carried in procession. It must be noted that the width of the stall is so narrow that two persons would have difficulty in sitting side by side.

In the garden of Great Canfield post office, Mr. Roe noticed two seats which were probably made for later Flitch ceremonies.

CHAPTER X

THE TOMBS AT LITTLE DUNMOW

No book on the Flitch would be complete without some refer. ence to the tombs at Little Dunmow as several writers have suggested that the FitzWalters should have all the credit for instituting the custom.

Of the many tombs which must have graced this priory church in its heyday, only two of any importance remain, and they are sadly mutilated. Both are between the slender, late twelfth-century columns of the former presbytery which, with the Lady Chapel, now serves as the parish church (see *Plates II, III*) so hideous externally, but with much rich carving within. Many stories have been told of these two monuments, and as would be expected, a legend has grown up which connects them with the Flitch.

The older and easternmost tomb (see *Plate IV*) is made up of an alabaster recumbent effigy of a lady in a sideless gown and a corded cloak ; about her throat is an elaborate lace collar decorated with jewels, and round her neck a Lancastrian collar of SS. A small cap, with a central jewel and lappets behind, covers her head which rests on a cushion supported by two angels ; at her feet are two little dogs. Her hands, with eleven rings, are in an attitude of prayer. The figure lies upon an altar-tomb of Purbeck marble panelled on the north and south sides, and east end, with diagonal cusped panels which formerly had brasses on the now blank shields; the west end of the tomb is plain. Tradition asserts that the lady is none other than the Fair Matilda, daughter of Sir Robert FitzWalter (see below), but no such extravagant claim can be entertained. The altar-tomb may be ascribed to the late fifteenth century, while the effigy is undoubtedly that of Joan Devereux, wife of Walter, Lord FitzWalter, who died on 10 or 11 May, 1409, aged about 29. Thus it would appear that the base of Lady FitzWalter's tomb having been destroyed, her figure was put on that of an unknown person who died towards the end of the same century. Walter, Lord Fitz-Walter had an adventurous career ; he was born at Henham on 5th

September, 1368 and, like many men of his day, saw armed service abroad. While on a voyage from Rome to Naples he was captured by Saracen pirates, imprisoned at Tunis, ransomed by Genoese merchants, and died at Venice on 16th May 1406. His young widow, whose mother was Margaret, daughter of John de Vere, Earl of Oxford, married Sir Hugh Burnell, of Holdgate, Shropshire, just over a year later, and he survived her by eleven years.

The second tomb (see *Plate XXVIII*), further to the west, supports the alabaster figure of a man in plate armour with a mail standard and skirt, collar of SS. with 'tireth' pendant, and an elaborate hip-belt; his head, with 'bobbed' hair, rests on his helmet from which most of the crest, apparently a snake, is broken. The feet of the figure are missing, as is the head of the lion on which they rested. By his side is his lady in a long gown, a corded cloak, and a richly ornamented horned head-dress ; angels were originally supporters of her pillow, and she too, has little dogs at her feet. The man wears many finger-rings, but his wife's small hands are broken off ; she has an elaborate necklace. These damaged figures lie on the remains of an alabaster tomb with fragments of three panels on the south side. One of these compartments has a shield suspended from a Tudor rose and carrying the arms of Cobham impaling Chidiok and FitzWarin quarterly, another has the arms of Cobham, and the third shows the bare legs and feet of a figure. At the eastern end of the tomb is a naked bearded figure holding a shield on which the arms of FitzWalter impaling Chidiok and FitzWarin quarterly may be discerned.

From these arms, and the style of the costumes, we are able to identify this as the tomb of Walter, Lord FitzWalter (son of the lady whose monument is described above) and his wife Elizabeth, daughter of Sir John Chidiok. Walter was born at Woodham Walter on 22 June, 1400 or 1401, and died on 25 November, 1431. He was the second husband of Elizabeth Chidiok (she being the widow of William Massey), and she took, as her third husband, Sir Thomas Cobham of Sterborough, Surrey, which accounts for the Cobham arms on this tomb.

Other members of the FitzWalter family known or believed to have been buried in Little Dunmow priory are :

(1)   Walter FitzRobert, 1198.
(2)   Robert FitzWalter, 1235 ; son of (1).
(3)   Sir Robert FitzWalter, 1325/6 ; grandson of (2).
(4)   Devorguille (de Burgh), 1284 ; first wife of (3).

PLATE XXVII

OFFICERS AND CLAIMANTS AT THE 1897 'TRIAL'.

1. Edmund Piper, draper. 2. A. J. Mills, corn and coal merchant. 3. John Brazier, painter and decorator. 4. W. G. Linsell. 5. James Hamilton, sanitary inspector. 6. Frank Hamilton (brother of James). 7. Charles J. Butcher, agricultural engineer. 8. T. Gibbons, brewer. 9. John Pepper, builder. 10. Philip Buck, baker. 11. Frederick Lewis, hardwareman. 12. John Wright, farmer.
13. Josiah Lambert } of Mildmay Road, Islington, London.   15. Eliza Tayler } of Little Leighs, Essex.
14. Mary Lambert }   16. George Tayler }

PLATE XXVIII

The Tomb of Walter, Lord FitzWalter (died 1431), and Elizabeth (Chidiok) his Wife, in Little Dunmow Priory Church

(5) Alianore (de Ferrers), before 1308 ; second wife of (3).
(6) Walter FitzRobert, 1293 ; son of (3) and (4).
(7) Joan (de Multon), 1363 ; wife of Sir Robert FitzWalter who was son of (3) and (5).
(8) John Lord FitzWalter, 1361 ; son of (7).
(9) Alianore (de Percy), died before 1361 ; wife of (8).
(10) Alianore (de Bohun), died after 1375 ; first wife of Walter, Lord FitzWalter who was son of (8) and (9).
(11) Joan (Devereux), 1409 ; wife of Walter, Lord FitzWalter who was son of (10).
(12) Walter, Lord FitzWalter, 1431 ; son of (11).
(13) Elizabeth (Chidiok), 1464 ; wife of (12).

Whether or not either of the ancient stone coffin-lids remaining in the priory church ever covered the remains of Lady Juga Baynard or of the Fair Matilda is open to conjecture. The story of the struggle between King John and Matilda (daughter of that strenuous knight, Sir Robert FitzWalter, who with Stephen Langton behind him, forced the *Magna Carta* from the King) has no place in this history ; the inquisitive reader will find it repeated in many books, but nowhere more graphically than Thomas Fuller's version in his *Worthies of England*.

King John and Matilda, a tragedy by Robert Davenport acted in 1651, included the lines :

FitzWalter. Good King John, weep, weep very heartily ;
　　　　　　It will become you sweetly. At your eyes
　　　　　　Your sin stole in ; there pay your sacrifice.
John. Back unto Dunmow Priory. There we'll pay
　　　　To sweet Matilda's memory, and her sufferings,
　　　　A monthly obsequy, which (sweet'ned by
　　　　The wealthy woes of a tear-troubled eye)
　　　　Shall by those sharp afflictions of my face
　　　　Court mercy, and make grief arrive at grace.

On the wall to the north of the altar is a tablet to the memory of Sir Robert, " Founder of our Civil Liberty, Marshall of the Army of God and of His Church ", set up in the seven hundredth year from the sealing of the Great Charter near the grave " before the High Altar of the Priory Church which he re-edified and adorned ". An attempt to locate FitzWalter's tomb was made in 1914.

On the north wall of the sanctuary is the large monument to the Hallett family who were lords of the manor for many generations ; their arms, *Or, a chief engrailed sable, over all on a bend gules, three bezants,* and crest, *Out of a ducal coronet or, a demi-lion rampant argent, holding in the paws a bezant,* are at the top. The Hallett motto, *Nil nisi jurantibus* (Nothing unless you are able to swear) seems singularly appropriate for a family connected with the Flitch awards.

Just before leaving Little Dunmow church, the visitor may care to see the pig carved on a spandrel of the arcading in the south wall ; this little porker, looking particularly happy, is nothing to do with the Flitch custom as he is in the company of other farmyard animals, with a wyvern, squirrel, cat, dog, and grotesque human figures, all of late fourteenth-century date, and of great interest.

CHAPTER XI

SOME MORE SONGS AND RHYMES CONNECTED WITH THE FLITCH

In addition to the verses quoted in Chapter III, the following, of doubtful literary merit, are included as a record ; most of them are of nineteenth-century date :

THE DUNMOW FLITCH

Words by S. Colborn.   Music by A. G. Colborn.

Published in Vol. 12 of *Beecham's Portfolio*.

A fig for a bachelor's life, I say,
For I've been married a year today,
That day was the happiest of my life,
When I made little Betsy Bell my wife.
My Betsy is a sweet little dove,
And each other we most truly love ;
Who loves most I don't know which,
So we're going to try for the Dunmow Flitch.

Chorus :

Oh ! the Dunmow Flitch ! the Dunmow Flitch !
We shall get it, that is certain, for there can't be a hitch,
And poor piggy little thinks, as he takes his forty winks,
That they're feeding him up for the Dunmow Flitch.

We're happy as little birds on the green trees,
In wishes and thoughts " As like as two peas ",
" For better, for worse ", we never fall out,
So the flitch we shall gain, there isn't a doubt.
Oh ! what dainty dishes my Betsy will make,
Nice rashers of bacon when the flitch we take.
Oh ! savoury piggy I'm longing for you,
To toast you or boil you or eat you in stew.

Chorus :

Oh ! the Dunmow Flitch ! etc.

Ev'ry day after work Betsy sits by my side ;
She's my own little comforter, darling and guide,
When lost for a word she will give me the hint,
Oh ! I wouldn't be single ! No ! not for the Mint !
Why Betsy, my love, there's a bang at the door !
Halloa ! where am I ? Why flat on the floor.
Out of bed I have tumbled, so it would seem,
And still I'm a bachelor, 'twas only a dream.

Chorus :

Oh ! the Dunmow Flitch ! the Dunmow Flitch !
We shall lose it, that is certain, for there comes the hitch,
And poor piggy, in his sty, can " wink the other eye ,
Now he knows he won't be wanted for the Dunmow Flitch.

Harrison Ainsworth's version of the origin of the Flitch
Custom as given in *The Flitch of Bacon* (1854) :

The Custom of Dunmow.
Showing how it arose.

Fytte the First.
A Fond Couple make a Vow before the Good
Prior of the Convent of our Lady of Dunmow,
that they have loved each other well and truly for
a Twelvemonth and a Day ; and crave his
Blessing.

I

" What seek you here, my children dear ?
Why kneel ye down thus lowly
Upon the stones, beneath the porch
Of this our Convent holy ? "
The Prior old the pair bespoke
In faltering speech, and slowly.

II

Their modest garb would seem proclaim
The pair of low degree,
But though in cloth of frieze arrayed,
A stately youth was he ;
While she, who knelt down by his side,
Was beautiful to see.

III

" A Twelvemonth and a Day have fled
    Since first we were united ;
And from that hour ", the young man said,
    " No change our hopes has blighted.
Fond faith with fonder faith we've paid
    And love with love requited.

IV

" True to each other have we been ;
    No dearer object seeing,
Than each has in the other found ;
    In everything agreeing.
And every look, and word, and deed
    That breed dissension fleeing.

V

" All this we swear, and take in proof
    Our Lady of Dunmow !
For She, who sits with saints above,
    Well knows that it is so.
Attest our Vow, thou reverend man,
    And bless us ere we go ! "

VI

The Prior old stretch'd forth his hands ;
    " Heaven prosper ye ! " quoth he ;
" O'er such as ye, right gladly we
    Say ' Benedicite ! ' "
On this, the kneeling pair uprose—
    Uprose full joyfully.

Fytte the Second.
Good Prior merrily bestoweth a Boon upon the
Loving Couple ; and getteth a noble
Recompense.

I

Just then, pass'd by the Convent cook—
    And moved the young man's glee ;
On his broad back a mighty Flitch
    Of Bacon brown bore he.
So heavy was the load, I wis,
    It scarce mote carried be.

II

" Take ye that Flitch," the Prior cried,
    " Take it, fond pair, and go ;
Fidelity, like yours, deserves
    The boon I now bestow.
Go, feast your friends, and think upon
    The Convent of Dunmow."

III

" Good Prior," then the youth replied,
    " Thy gift to us is dear,
Not for its worth, but that it shows
    Thou deem'st our love sincere,
And in return broad lands I give—
    Broad lands thy Convent near ;
Which shall to thee and thine produce
    A Thousand Marks a year !

IV

" But this Condition I annex,
    Or else the Grant's forsaken ;
That whensoe'er a pair shall come,
    And take the Oath we've taken,
They shall from thee and thine receive
    A goodly Flitch of Bacon.

V

" And thus from out a simple chance
    A usage good shall grow ;
And our example of true love
    Be held up evermo :
While all who win the prize shall bless
    The Custom of Dunmow."

VI

" Who art thou, son ? " the Prior cried,
    His tones with wonder falter—
" Thou should'st not jest with reverend men,
    Nor with their feelings palter."
" I jest not, Prior, for know in me
    Sir Reginald Fitzwalter.

VII

"I now throw off my humble garb,
    As I what I am, confest ;
The wealthiest I of wealthy men,
    Since with this treasure blest."
And as he spoke, Fitzwalter clasp'd
    His lady to his breast.

VIII

"In peasant guise my love I won,
    Nor knew she whom she wedded ;
In peasant cot our truth we tried,
    And no disunion dreaded.
Twelve months' assurance proves our faith
    On firmest base is steadied."

IX

Joy reigned within those Convent walls
    When the glad news was known ;
Joy reigned within Fitzwalter's halls
    When there his bride was shown.
No lady in the land such sweet
    Simplicity could own ;
A natural grace had she, that all
    Art's graces far outshone :
Beauty and worth for want of birth
    Abundantly atone.

L'ENVOY

Hence the Custom.

What need of more ?   That Loving **Pair**
    Lived long and truly so ;
Nor ever disunited were ;—
    For one death laid them low !
And hence arose that Custom old—
    The Custom of Dunmow.

The broadsheet, illustrated on p. 52, may be dated to the 1855 ceremony because of the references to the Frenchman, M. de Chatelain, who was one of the claimants, and to the war with Russia at the time.

In addition to the broadsheet illustrated on p. 44, there were two others decorated with woodcuts (see *Plate XVI*, and *Fig. 5*). The words on that with the two yokels (*Plate XVI*) refer, in passing, to the police officer and his wife who were claimants at the ' trials ' held on 25 June 1857 :

ESSEX

Dunmow and Bacon

YOU Essex LADS and LASSES all,
    So handsome, gay, and jolly,
By wind and steam away they go,
    From country Town and City.
There's twenty thousand old and young,
    If I am not mistaken.
With a loud huzza !—this glorious day,
    We will claim this flitch of bacon.

CHORUS.

    Thus married be love—and agree,
        And if I'm not mistaken,
    You may next year to Dunmow steer,
        And claim the flitch of bacon.

Pretty Mary leaves her cow,
    And off she goes so mellow,
Buxom Johnny leaves his plough,
    And trips across the meadows,
O'er the stiles and up the lanes,
    They will not be mistaken,
For Johnny says, to pretty Jane—
    " I wish I had the Bacon."

There's Dick the snob, and Metfield Bob,
    And pretty Stratford Mary,
So plump and flat in Jack Shepherd hat,
    Goes over the fields so airy.
Next week, says she, " we'll married be,"
    Love shall not be forsaken,
There is nothing beats [*sic*]
    And a lump of Dunmow Bacon.

A Farmer does at Stanstead live
    A very rum old joker,
He swore his wife he would well wop,
    With the shovel and the poker,
They were fighting like a dog and cat,
    And such a row was making,
The old woman said, love, " I am afraid—
    You'll never get the Bacon."

Now a Policeman[1] people say,
    One, who is a Detector—
From Nottingham did sneak away,
    What a very fine Inspector,
With his lov'ng wife, so free from strife,
    I'm sure I'm not mistaken,
With his rolling pin now he will sing—
    We have gained the flitch of bacon.

[1]Thomas Jerimiah Heard of Staffordshire, not Nottingham, as stated (see p. 36).

The twenty fifth of June the girls in bloom,
    From every part will run now,
Huzza ! huzza ! this glorious day
    We'll see the rigs of Dunmow.
The couples on men's shoulders placed
    All through the town are taken ;
We will drink and sing, the bells shall ring
    Here is Dunmow lads and bacon.

Now as the pretty maids went home,
    From Dunmow blythe and bonny,
Little Jenny said to Sam,
    And Mary said to Johnny,
I wish that we had married been,
    I am sure we should have taken
This glorious day, in Dunmow Town
    The stunning flitch of Bacon.

The bells shall ring, and we will sing
    The twenty-fifth of June now,
And recollect until we die
    The glorious sights of Dunmow.

The scene (*Fig.* 5) of a wife about to strike her unfaithful husband decorated a broadsheet printed for the 1857 ceremony by W. Dever, of 18 Great Saint Andrew St., Broad Street, Bloomsbury.

One verse of a song by George Marsham Tweddell, F.S.A.Scot., with music by Leopold Wagner, specially composed for the 1877 ceremony, brings to mind the typical music-hall artiste of the days before the First World War :

The custom was an honoured one
In ages long gone by ;
'Twas kept by brave and loving hearts
That 'neath the sod now lie.
'Twas good for them—'tis good for us ;
And when we, too, are gone,
It will be prized by loving pairs
When two hearts beat in one.
For Dunmow's flitch they've honour more
Than warriors' laurels drenched in gore.

(Quoted in *The Morning Advertiser* and *The Chelmsford Chronicle,* 27 July, 1877).

EPILOGUE

And so this brief history of the famous Custom of Dunmow comes to an end, and the reader will no doubt be surprised at the small number of unquestionable statements which can be found concerning it. The aim of the book has been to record all that can be verified about an English institution which has become known the world over. Some who have had patience to read this account may be able to add a little to it ; a few will blame me for suggesting that certain long-cherished beliefs are based on false premises. Perhaps other readers will say that the story would have been better terminated with the account of the 1751 ceremony.

Even if the ceremony has degenerated into a travesty of its former self, the idea behind it need not be lightly dismissed. Whether the origin of awarding bacon to happy couples be deemed pagan or Christian, or merely the adaptation of a pagan custom to meet Christian ideals, those few who applied for it in the first six centuries of its recorded history solemnly believed in the righteousness of their claims, and it would be wrong to belittle the faith of those who could take an oath with the conviction that perjury was not being committed.

While we leave this old Essex custom to the mercy of cartoonists, advertisers, modern 'judges, juries and counsel', to the wireless, the television and the cinema, we can be sure that the 'trials' arranged under the auspices of an efficient local committee instead of commercial showmen will be conducted with decency and regard to the thought behind them.

To be judged worthy of the Flitch is a compliment which married couples envy either secretly or openly, and a rhyme which appeared on a card issued in 1855 seems an appropriate note on which to finish :

> It were well if " our custom " so widely was spread,
> That every fond couple resolved to be wed ;
> Would determine to please, to charm and bewitch,
> That in *any Year*, they might each claim the Flitch.
>
> Should this be the case, a glad World would be ours,
> The thorns and the briars would bloom into flowers,
> And all might rejoice, the poor and the rich,
> If all would *deserve*, and lay claim to the Flitch.